All for Christ

BY THE SAME AUTHOR

Backward Christian Soldiers
Orphans of the Living

All for Christ

Some Twentieth Century Martyrs

DIANA DEWAR

Oxford New York Toronto Melbourne

OXFORD UNIVERSITY PRESS

1980

Oxford University Press, Walton Street, Oxford OX2 6DP
OXFORD LONDON GLASGOW
NEW YORK TORONTO MELBOURNE WELLINGTON
KUALA LUMPUR SINGAPORE JAKARTA HONG KONG TOKYO
DELHI BOMBAY CALCUTTA MADRAS KARACHI
NAIROBI DAR ES SALAAM CAPE TOWN

British Library Cataloguing in Publication Data
Dewar, Diana
All for Christ.
1.   *Christian martyrs – Biography*
1.   *Title*
272   BR1601.2   79–42709
ISBN 0-19-213115-X
ISBN 0-19-283024-4 Pbk

Printed in Great Britain by
Cox & Wyman Ltd, Reading

Foreword

by Leslie Brown, Bishop of Uganda 1953–61, Archbishop 1961–65

The first martyrdom recorded in this book is that of Archbishop Luwum in February 1977. There is no doubt that the Archbishop's death was a genuine martyrdom. He died because he refused to confess to a crime he had not committed. In April 1976 I had been with him at a conference in Trinidad. I asked him about the prospects for the Church under Amin's rule. He said that one thing was plain. Christians must refuse to compromise the truth and, as they stood firm, some would undoubtedly be killed. His prophecy was fulfilled in his own death, less than a year afterwards.

As Mrs. Dewar reminds us in this book, it is rare nowadays for a Christian to be condemned on the ground of his faith. Some alleged crime, political or otherwise, is almost always the ostensible reason for his death. Sometimes, too, it is very hard to sift out the truth, as is well illustrated in the account of Ivan Moiseyev.

The twentieth century has produced many witnesses to the truth of Christ. Chinese Christians died because of friendship with foreign missionaries, German and Dutch Christians died protesting against injustice or Hitler's treatment of the Jews, thousands have died for their rejection of atheist philosophy. In our life-time martyrs for Christ, known or unknown, are innumerable.

Sometimes we all ask whether the sacrifice of so many noble human beings achieves any good, for martyrdoms seem never to end. Occasionally, when we know all the facts, the effect of a martyrdom is evident. Archbishop Luwum's death did not destroy faith in the loving purpose of God; it spread and confirmed that faith. The question we ask about the death of the martyrs we also ask about the death of Christ, and in this case believers know the effect of that complete self-giving on them and on the world.

Mrs. Dewar has done the Church a considerable service in writing this book. It will inspire and strengthen every Christian who reads it.

For Bob, with love

Contents

Photographs of the martyrs will be found near the centre of the book

For whosoever will save his life shall lose it:
and whosoever will lose his life for my sake shall find it.

Matthew 16: 25.

Janani Luwum

1924–1977

The twentieth century may account for more martyrs than the sum of preceding centuries. Their witness ought to be honoured and preserved to inspire the faithless and rally the faithful, but the records are neglected. The stories of men and women are told here to represent a multitude of unknown modern martyrs. Unlike Janani Luwum, Ugandan Archbishop, they are unheralded, although many have also been moved by their Christian constancy to similarly unequivocal protest when loyalty to oppressive government conflicted with duty to Christ.

Summoned by the drum rolls over the Kampala valley, the people toiled up the steep hill to the great red-brick cathedral on its summit. The cathedral, astride the wistfully-named Hill of Peace, the highest of the seven hills which cordon the capital, has its own theatrical history. The first building was blown down in a hurricane. The second, known as the 'forest of poles', was pulled down, and the third destroyed by fire. The copper dome and cross of the fourth cathedral glinted under the immaculate sun of this special day, and both symbolized the shining, steely faith of the three thousand people who filled Namirembe Cathedral for morning service. Four days had passed since the dramatic death of their beloved Archbishop.

Janani Luwum and two cabinet ministers died while they were detained by the security forces. The official story claimed that the three men lost their lives in a road smash as they attempted to overcome the driver of an army vehicle taking them for interrogation.

The rightful burial place for the Archbishop was here in the shadow of the cathedral. Brother bishops had arranged his funeral; but there was no body.

The Minister of Health's promise to the bishops had been, 'You can have the body after Government investigation.' Next day it was 'a matter for the military'. The Military Secretary told them, 'The Archbishop's body has been taken to his home in the north for private burial.' The Primate could not be buried like that, the bishops protested. 'Bring us the body,' they pleaded. 'If you can't, give us permission to get the body ourselves.' Suddenly, the whole affair was 'in the hands of the President'. The bishops were warned to ask no more about it.

The decree was 'No memorial service'. Perhaps the Government feared that a public show of grief might put the spark of anger to Amin's tinder-dry presidential throne; but the official ruling did not prevent an ordinary Sunday morning service and it was to turn into a celebration of the life and witness of Luwum.

The customary service was followed by Holy Communion and many of the country's bishops stood for more than an hour giving the bread and the wine. The congregation was tense and at the altar rail the words, 'Take this . . . in remembrance that Christ died for thee . . . preserve thy body and soul . .' took on unusual and urgent meaning. The priests were praying for the lives of the believers.

At last the people came out to stand on the green precincts around the cathedral. The rays of the sun illuminated the depths of the empty grave and Mary of Mucwini, the widow of the Arch-bishop, wept as had another Mary. Spontaneously, the people, robbed not only of the body but of the opportunity to express their inmost emotions, began to sing.

> 'Daily, daily sing the praises
> Of the city God hath made;
> In the beauteous fields of Eden.
> Its foundation-stones are laid.'

It was the first verse of the Swahili hymn, 'Killa Siku Tuusifu', sung by three boy martyrs, the first Ugandans to die for their faith more than a hundred years ago. The hymn swelled in the still air and the lilting chorus rose again and again as a paean of praise for the delights of heaven.

> 'O, that I had wings of angels
> Here to spread and heavenward fly;
> I would seek the gates of Sion
> Far beyond the starry sky!'

The indestructible message of the angels that first Easter Day, 'He is not here . . . He is risen' was given the mourners by Archbishop Erica Sabiti, Luwum's predecessor, who was heard to say, 'Why are we bothering about the body?' The hilltop reverberated with the hymn of the balokole ('saved ones'), 'Tukutendereza Yesu'.

> 'Glory, glory, hallelujah!
> Glory, glory to the Lamb!
> O, the cleansing blood has reached me!
> Glory, glory to the Lamb!'

Then more familiar Easter hymns soared from the great crowd thronging around the open grave dug beside the burial place of James Hannington, the first martyred bishop of Uganda, who came from England, and was speared dead on the threshold of the country.

There, on this Sunday, a sense of history suffused the occasion and the multitude lifted their voices under the open sky in commemoration of another bishop, Luwum.

*

The Archbishop's household was asleep. Built in the elbow of the Hill of Peace, which falls away from the cathedral, the red-brick modern house has a character lent by changes of level due to its position. A comfortable home, more looked after by family than servants, it could be reached from the Provincial Office of the Archbishop through gardens flamboyant with bougainvilleas, orchids and paradise bird flowers. Recently, as violence grew in Uganda, the gates had been locked at night, and visitors needed to telephone to arrange entry.

A commotion aroused the Luwums in the early hours of Saturday, February 5, 1977, and a man, seemingly in great distress, was heard outside shouting for help. The Archbishop could not ignore such a cry. He opened his doors and, as he emerged, found he had been duped. The wire fence around the compound was broken and soldiers, using as a decoy a Langi tribesman named Ben Ongom, a businessman from Lira in the north, whom they had arrested and tortured, inveigled the Archbishop to come out. Armed men sprang up before him and demanded arms. 'What arms?' asked the Archbishop. The answer was the muzzle of a rifle pressed against his stomach by the Arabic-speaking leader, while another man frisked him. The soldiers then searched the house exhaustively. They even looked underneath the Holy Table in the Chapel. They rummaged the food stores, putting their hands into sacks of sesame seed, millet, and groundnuts.

At one point Ben Ongom, who was handcuffed, pleaded, 'Please help us. If the arms are not here tell us the location of any Acholi or Langi homes in Namirembe so that they may be searched.' An Acholi himself, the Archbishop knew that both these tribes were considered enemies to the Military Government. He told Ongom sternly that he had not come to Namirembe for the Acholi or the Langi. He said with dignity, 'I am the Archbishop of Uganda, Rwanda, Burundi and Boga-Zaire, and there are no arms in my house. Our house is God's house. We pray for the President. We pray for the security forces whatever they do. We preach the gospel and pray for others. That is our work, not keeping arms.'

Only after they had ransacked every room and found nothing incriminating did the soldiers leave. The Archbishop opened the compound gates for them himself.

He was deeply troubled. He was not a man given to heroics, nor did he 'meddle in politics', but over the past month he had become increasingly aware of the threat to his own life. Despite his protests about the régime Janani Luwum had continued to attend Government functions because, he told his people, 'The President needs friends. We must love the President. We must pray for him.' His charity persuaded some he was on the Government side but in December, 1976, Luwum told one of his critics, 'I do not know for how long I shall be occupying this chair. I live as though there will be no tomorrow. I face daily being picked up by the soldiers.'

A devoted family man (his wife had given him eight children), his work always came first; he saw himself as Christ's man on the spot. 'Even if I have to die for my convictions,' he told a friend, 'I can never lower the standards God has set me.' A favourite text when he preached came from the challenging words in Romans, Chapter 12: 'I beseech you therefore, brethren, by the mercies of God, that ye present your bodies a living sacrifice ... And be not conformed to this world: but be ye transformed by the renewing of your mind, that ye may prove what is that good, and accept-able, and perfect, will of God.'

As he prayed for his Lord's orders in battle, he felt the weight of the sorrows of the nation. Often tears would well in his eyes when he remembered another of his friends who had 'disappeared'. The powerful physique of the Archbishop spoke of his inheritance. It was his tribe, the Acholi, and the Langi, both in the north, and predominantly Christian, who suffered the brunt of the Army's brutality. The deposed President, Milton Obote, an exile in neighbouring Tanzania, was a Langi. Both the Acholi and Langi are traditionally warrior tribes of strong tall men who since the days of first colonization had been the backbone of the Army and the police.

President Amin suspected that any opposition to his rule would come from among these two northern tribes who were known to be politically alert, and he was convinced that the Acholi and the Langi had engineered the Entebbe raid in July 1976. 'We did not do very well,' he told his ministers at the time, 'because the Acholi and Langi officers were in contact with the Israelis.'

As the numbers of widows and orphans increased in the churches, so the Archbishop began to feel it was his duty to do more than to bury the dead and to comfort those who mourned. Lately he had felt older than his half century and it showed in his face: the creases made by his capacious smile were augmented by contours of shared griefs and anxieties.

The Archbishop was careful never to criticize the Government when out of the country, even to friends; and at home he preached support for the President in 'all that was good'. He valued his friendship with the President; but he urged people to follow Christian principles even if this meant defying authority.

The latest incident had brought Amin's soldiers to his door. It seemed to the Archbishop to focus the conflict between his duty to God and his allegiance to the Government. His feeling of crisis was intensified next day by news of the arrest of Bishop Yona Okoth of Bukedi, of the Mudama tribe who live in the south-east district bordering Kenya and are closely related to the Acholi and Langi. Bishop Okoth was released only when nothing incriminating could be found at his personal or official residences. Ben Ongom was again forced to play the role of decoy. Again the soldiers demanded to see arms. The bishop showed them a shotgun for which he had a licence. When they asked for other arms, he said, 'I look after the church, I do not look after guns.'

Janani Luwum could hesitate no longer. He convened an extraordinary meeting of the House of Bishops, and he thanked God he could rely on his 'brothers' rallying to make decisions together and to act in unison, because the character of the Ugandan church remained remarkable for its strength of fellowship.

Immediately, in response to his telephone calls, the bishops came from all parts of the country to the Church Guest House on the Hill of Peace to discuss the two incidents. Later, they set down their grievances and concerns for the Church and for the nation in a letter to the President, dated 10 February 1977.

Signed by the Archbishop and countersigned by fifteen brother bishops, the letter was innocent of political manoeuvre but uncompromising in Christian content. Its tone was strong, yet respectful, and facts were presented as the bishops saw them.

The Christians are asking, 'If this is what is happening to our bishops, then where are we?' The gun, whose muzzle has been pressed against the Archbishop's stomach, the gun used to search the Bishop of Bukedi's houses, is a gun pointed at every Christian in the Church . . .

The security of the ordinary Christian has been in jeopardy for quite a long time. It may be that what has happened to the Archbishop and the Bishop of Bukedi is a climax of what is consistently happening to our Christians. We have buried many who have died as a result of being shot and there are many more whose bodies have not been found. Their disappearance is connected with the activities of some members of the security forces. If it is required we can give concrete evidence of what is happening because widows and orphans are members of our Church.

The House of Bishops were careful in their choice of words. Behind the arguments over shades of meaning, the Archbishop saw distraught people who came to his office daily to implore help. No one must be turned away. He was adamant that he would see anyone, beggars, students, refugees, frightened women. Only yesterday a woman at the office had wept and said, 'I've not seen my husband for a week. I don't know where he is. I think he's been picked up by the police.' The secret police did not wear uniform but dressed ostentatiously, typically in flowered shirts, bell-bottomed trousers, dark glasses.

'People come first, papers second,' he told Sylvia, his pretty dark-haired secretary, sent out by the Church Missionary Society in England, who would be chafing to deal with the correspondence. Unfailingly, the Archbishop made his visitors feel that at that moment they were the very people he wanted to meet, and he always made time to try to reach the truth with them. He would go to the limits to help. He could call on cabinet ministers, ask to see the President himself.

Recently he had found his approaches useless. In the past the President had assured the bishops of his readiness to meet them and he had even given the Archbishop a secret telephone number so that he could be contacted wherever he might be in the country. Now this 'hot line' had been cut, and the gap between the Christian leaders and the Government had become a chasm. The bishops were specific in their letter about their concern.

We had been assured by you of your ready availability to religious leaders whenever they had serious matters to discuss with you. You had even gone to the extent of giving His Grace, the Archbishop, the surest means of contacting you in this country wherever you may be. But a situation has developed now where you have become more and more inaccessible to the Archbishop and even when he tried to write he has not received any reply.

They reminded the President that he had said publicly, and on many occasions, that religious leaders had a special place in the country because of their cloth and he treated them with respect. 'You have on many occasions publicly demonstrated this and we are always grateful.'

Relations *had* been cordial and the Archbishop recalled how he and the President would often chat and share a joke in public. By disposition Janani Luwum had a joyous faith and a bubbling sense of humour. He loved music. He played the African drum and he liked to sing. His warm tenor voice was attractive, and only lack of time prevented him joining the Kampala Singers, as did his young English secretary from Barnard Castle in Yorkshire.

Frequently the Archbishop would say to the President, 'We are with you, Your Excellency, with all that you do that is good.' But last December the bishops had been shocked to hear the President say that some of them had preached bloodshed. The Archbishop's own Christmas broadcast, proclaiming that the only true victory was that of suffering love, had been cut short because it was construed as 'political comment'. 'We waited anxiously to be called by Your Excellency to clarify such a serious situation, but all in vain.'

The House of Bishops also expressed their sadness at the increasing forces that set Ugandans against each other. The President was a somewhat idiosyncratic Muslim and they protested that Muslim candidates were preferred for leading positions in the State. They also alleged that some members of Islam were using their rank to coerce Christians into becoming Muslims. The Ugandan Muslims number perhaps half-a-million among the population of eleven millions while there are some eight million Christians. A report was circulating that Amin had made a deal with Libya to convert Uganda from a Christian to a Muslim State. Increasingly the President had turned to the Islamic States for help. President Muammar el-Qaddafi of Libya told Amin, 'You are a prophet! I see another Mohammed. Be brave and we will support you!' This was broadcast on Uganda Radio. King Faisal of Saudi Arabia gave Amin a golden sword, adjuring him, 'With this sword make your country Muslim.' Amin was attempting to cancel the centenary celebrations of the Church of Uganda and records relating to Church property were being destroyed.

The first Christian missionaries had arrived in the kingdom of Buganda, the precursor of Uganda, a hundred years before. They came at the invitation of Buganda's tribal king, Kabaka Mutesa I, who may have wanted them as a counterbalance to the Muslim threat from the coast and the expanding Egyptian empire to the north.

The Archbishop had designated 1977, the centenary year of the Church of Uganda, a Year of Christian Mobilization. Much of the crusading contribution of the past was no longer needed because Ugandan Christians had assumed the work, but missionaries were still wanted for service in the theological colleges, industrial mission teams, and to help development projects. More and more people were being baptized and confirmed, and the Archbishop was never happier than when conducting a confirmation tour.

He was zealous to promote education and was only too aware of the shortcomings of some of the converts. He had just made a cassette for the C.M.S., confessing: 'We realize that we have baptized and confirmed many who have remained babies in their faith.' He added, 'Let's use the media to motivate and teach so that Africans can become more responsible and effective Christians.'

The passage in the letter to Amin which deplored 'a war against the educated' came from the Archbishop's heart.

There is also a war against the educated that is forcing many of our people to run away from this country in spite of what the country has paid to educate them. This brain drain, the fear and the mistrust, make development, progress and stability almost impossible.

The letter went on dangerously,

While you have stated on the national radio that your Government is not under any foreign influence and that your decisions are guided by your Defence Council and Cabinet, the general trend of things in Uganda has created a feeling that the affairs of our nation are being directed by outsiders who do not have the welfare of this country and the value of the lives and properties of Ugandans at their hearts.

The bishops knew that Amin's army now consisted predominantly of foreigners, largely Nubians and Libyans. Some put the figure as high as 90 per cent. Amin himself came from a minority tribe, the Kakwa, who spill over the Sudanese border in the north and are themselves seen by some Ugandans as half-foreigners.

Many believed that the President had trained a court of 'tigers' now beyond control. Many atrocities were committed by a power-drunk Army without direct orders from a President who tried to rule with too much force and in turn had become a victim of runaway violence.

The bishops wrote,

The gun which was meant to protect Uganda as a nation, the Ugandan as a citizen and his property, is increasingly being used against the Ugandan to take away his life and his property. Many cars almost daily are being taken at gunpoint and their owners killed, and most of the culprits are never brought to justice. If required, we can enumerate many cases. Too much power has been given to members of State Research to arrest and kill at will innocent individuals.

The religious leaders knew it was impossible to present statistics about atrocities because those who did the killing were members of the innocently-named State Research Bureau, an infamous wing of the secret police. The uncertainty was largely due to the fact that casualties in the last six years were variously estimated at this time at between 30,000 and 300,000.

There were no reporters from the press of the Western world in the country now except at invitation of the President, and only Amnesty International documented the excesses of the military régime, mostly from the stories of refugees and newspaper correspondents in bordering countries. In Uganda rumours of 'disappearances', the common euphemism for murders, multiplied. There were also reports of arbitrary arrests, mass killings and refined torture. Routine methods of torture were alleged to include the ordering of prisoners to beat each other to death with hammers (the survivor is then shot), or to kill one another with car axles. In some detention centres cannibalism was said to have been enforced.

In recent weeks a new wave of atrocities had been concentrated on Christians, the professional classes, and the victimized Acholi and Lango tribespeople. Yet another of the countless 'plots' on the President's life was uncovered. This time it had been timed for January 25 (the anniversary of his own coup in 1971) when he was to open an agricultural show in Jinja, and it was purported to have been devised by Milton Obote and his supporters using Chinese-made weapons smuggled from Tanzania.

A girl spy was said by a British newspaper, the *Sunday Times*, to have smashed the plot by infiltrating meetings of the ringleaders, one of whom was arrested, tortured and killed. Whether she divulged many secrets under torture is unknown; but the President was alerted and news sources said that Amin drew up a death list of 7,000 in a revengeful pogrom, and refugees fleeing to Nairobi told of systematic massacres.

The bishops could see for themselves bodies floating in the rivers and lakes of their dramatically beautiful country. Corpses were also seen rotting in Luizira shipyard in Kampala and stuffed into drains.

The bishops' letter reminded the President that

The Archbishop is not only the Archbishop of the Church of Uganda but he is the Archbishop of the Church of Rwanda, Burundi and Boga-Zaire, so what happens to him here is also the concern of the Christians in Rwanda, Burundi and Zaire.

The Archbishop was thankful he was essentially a practical man because the problems of administering a community of three million Anglicans in a province which comprised four countries were formidable, particularly in view of the strong inherited tribal rivalries. He had become the symbol and instrument of unity and had succeeded in forging new friendships between the tribes. He preached the gospel and talked constantly of the power of love so effectively that no church was big enough to hold all those who wanted to hear him. Loudspeaker equipment and extra canopies outside to protect the overflowing congregation from the sun became routine necessities. Denominational differences were a burden to him and he worked hard to bring people together.

The letter continued:

In fact, it goes further than that because he is an Archbishop in the Anglican communion which is a worldwide community; so are the bishops.

An action such as this one [the search for arms of the bishops' houses] damages the good image of our nation. It also threatens our preparations for the centenary celebrations. Christians everywhere have become cautious about taking part in the fund-raising activities of the Church for fear of being misrepresented and misinterpreted.

The Archbishop knew Christians were being singled out in the persecution. Missionaries were expelled. There had been reports of Christian soldiers shot near Jinja when they disobeyed a ban on Army personnel attending midnight services. From Masaka came news that people wearing some of the 1¾ million special badges to commemorate the centenary of the Ugandan Church were burned to death. The President had attacked fund-raising functions for the centenary with insults. 'This was doing *magendo* [business] in church,' he sneered.

The bishops sat as a Council and took three days to compose their protest. They asked to see the President but were refused. On Saturday, February 12, half the bishops returned home while eight stayed in Kampala.

At midnight on Sunday the President telephoned the Archbishop to make angry accusations. Then, early on Monday morning, the Minister of Cabinet Affairs rang asking Luwum to go to the State House, Entebbe, at nine. A government car would fetch him. Mary, fearful for his safety, insisted on accompanying him. Amin insinuated that the Archbishop had been plotting with Obote to overthrow the Government because children had found arms near his home. Luwum told the President he did not contest the soldiers' right to search his house but objected to the method, by gunpoint in the middle of the night. He said the bishops had been trying all week to see him.

The President then became jovial. 'Don't worry about a thing! I will invite all the bishops to come and talk it over. I'll put them up in a hotel at my expense. How's that?'

The same day the bishops delivered their letter to the President. Realizing that its candour was likely to enrage him, and that he might try to suppress it, they arranged for copies of the letter to be smuggled out to Kenya. All Cabinet Ministers also received copies.

When Henry Kyemba (former Minister of Health, who defected to Britain on May 17 1977) received his copy he became certain that Amin would resolve to reassert his authority by murdering the Archbishop. He believed the President would stage-manage the production of faked evidence against 'conspirators', the chief of whom would be Luwum, and two Government Ministers 'who knew too much'.

The President replied to the bishops' protest the day after he received it. He summoned them to attend at the Conference Centre in Kampala on Wednesday, 16 February at 9.30 a.m. Amin wished to show to the religious leaders, diplomats, civil servants and others, the cache of weapons found by troops near the Archbishop's home. These weapons, it was said, were to have been used in a plot to kill him and to overthrow the régime. The Archbishop received the summons with a heavy heart, for he guessed that the President's advisers had become increasingly embarrassed and exasperated at his outspokenness and had counselled Amin to get rid of him.

*

The Archbishop did not need prophecy to realize that his future was precarious and he had spent much time and thought on providing for his family in the last year. He loved his wife and children dearly. The younger were normally exuberant, and not, as Sylvia, his secretary, once remarked, 'the least bit pious!' He was especially protective towards Mary, his wife, a sweet-natured unassuming woman who came from Mucwini, a small community in the deep bush in the northern region where Janani grew up as an ordinary peasant boy, helping his mother harvest the millet and tending his father's goats. His father was one of the earliest converts to Christianity among the Acholi and was a pioneer Christian worker and church teacher. Mary liked to busy herself with the meticulous care of her home and family. She was a little overawed by the role of Archbishop's wife in the capital, and shy partly because of her small command of English, but with Janani to look after her she was a happy woman.

The Archbishop worried about her asthma which had become worse since moving to Kampala. She had several spells in hospital and increasingly her distressing attacks prevented her accompanying him on official engagements. She had to cope with many problems, unexpected visitors and people coming to her husband with terrible stories of family members killed, imprisoned or disappearing. The Archbishop never returned from a trip away from home without a gift of some sort, a length of cloth perhaps, for 'my Mary'. Now he was thankful he had had the foresight to build more houses at Mucwini for Mary and the children and his numerous dependants. It was typical of him that he did not design palaces but round thatched huts, slightly more durable than the ordinary mud huts and so serving as an example of improved technology.

On the morning of their summons the bishops met first for prayers. The sun high in the sky was already hot and the airless day seemed to hold its breath. They drew up a memorandum denying all charges of complicity in plots. Then, wearing their cassocks and pectoral crosses, they left for the Conference Centre in the Nile Hotel, a couple of miles from Namirembe Hill. This was the last time Mary saw Janani, alive or dead.

Two friends accompanied the Archbishop in his car. They were the Dean of the Province, Bishop Silvanus Wani, who was also Protestant chaplain to the Army, and Bishop Festo Kivengere of Kigezi, Western Uganda. Outside the Nile Hotel, sitting in an enormous semi-circle, were at least two thousand troops in full uniform, their multi-coloured badges and belts representing different units drawn from all over the country. Spread out on the lawns in the centre of the gardens were the arms, automatic rifles, thousands of rounds of ammunition, grenades and sub-machine guns. According to Henry Kyemba who was present, they were all new

East-European weapons, exactly like those used by many units of the Ugandan Army and supplied to Ministers for official protection. Close by were the suitcases in which the arms were said to have been hidden, buried among clothes. Television cameras were in position and a bank of microphones set up for the speakers.

As well as eight bishops of the Anglican Church, led by Archbishop Luwum, there was the Roman Catholic Cardinal and the Muslim leader. The bishops had rough handling from some of the soldiers. 'You dog!' taunted one officer. They were made to stand for hours in the harsh sun while 'fellow-conspirators' read documents which implicated the Archbishop in the frustrated coup. Nothing in these statements implicated the two Cabinet Ministers, Mr. Charles Oboth Ofumbi, who was responsible for internal affairs, and Lt.-Col. Orinayo Wilson Oreyema, in charge of land and water resources. Both had worked closely with ex-President Obote, although at the time they appeared to support the coup, and were the last of the old guard. The others were now dead, exiled, or lying low in the rural areas of Uganda and had been replaced by army officers.

The President watched the proceedings from his offices above, pacing between the office balcony and the television set inside.

First of all, Colonel Isaac Malyamungu reminded the assembly that the Government had repeatedly warned of subversion. 'Here now is the proof of it.' Then followed statements by self-confessed conspirators of an attempt to topple Amin's régime. The first and longest was attributed to Dr. Milton Obote himself. It took Mr. Abdulla Anyuru, former chairman of the Public Service Commission, more than an hour to read, and it was extraordinarily similar to the bishops' letter. It described the misery of the people, how the President mismanaged the country, the harassment of ordinary people, and the slaughter. Kyemba observed, 'It was not, of course, from Obote. It was read direct from blue paper which was, I saw, the standard State House paper used for official documents.'

Near the end the Archbishop was implicated. Anti-Amin forces should be mobilized 'through people who cannot be suspected – like Archbishop Luwum and Bishop Yona Okoth of Bukedi'. The statement went on, 'Okoth, being near the border, can receive arms and pass them on to Kampala, so that Luwum can pass them on.'

Archbishop Luwum, a pre-eminent figure, standing six foot two, listened intently with his head slightly inclined to one side which was his manner when concentrating. Then he was seen to shake his head slowly in silent denial at the charges.

Two other statements followed from men who 'admitted' getting instructions from Obote, and receiving the arms on show. Lt. Ogwang of the Uganda Army said he had been approached by one of the conspirators and had given information about his unit, the Malire Mechanized Reconnaissance Regiment, near Kampala, where he was intelligence officer. The other 'confession' came from Ben Ongom, who had been used as a decoy by Amin's soldiers to force entry into the bishops' houses.

The Vice-President, General Mustafa Adrisi, had heard enough. He sprang up before the microphones and declared, 'I want you to judge these people here and now!' The soldiers had been given their cue. 'Kinja yeye! Kinja yeye! [Kill them! Kill them!]' they shouted hoarsely.

To the Archbishop the scene was like a bad play with crude and unlikely dialogue. Above all, he was a man of peace and his criticisms had always been constructive and peaceable.

Scheming was not in his nature and any suggestion of collusion with Dr. Obote was as probable as snow on Namirembe, for Obote was a thrusting politician who sometimes gave the impression that he was without much time for the Church and his relationships with Church leaders were deliberately tenuous. Many issues divided them. Anyway, politics was not the Archbishop's game. God's work was his business and it seemed as if it was finished.

He tried to keep up with the rapid and excited delivery of the Vice-President and then they were marshalled inside the Conference Centre and another senior officer was speaking. The religious leaders were ordered into an adjacent room, and the two cabinet ministers told to leave by another door, while the President addressed the Army. 'Control your tempers,' he told them. 'I want a proper military trial by a military court. It will be proper justice. The cases will be judged properly before any sentences are passed.'

Only when the meeting was over were the bishops told they

could go home. As the Archbishop was about to leave, a soldier seized him by the arm. 'You are wanted by the President to sign and discuss something in the next room.' Bishop Wani (now Archbishop) tried to go with him but was repelled at the door. 'I see the hand of the Lord in all this,' said Archbishop Luwum.

The bishops waited by the Archbishop's car for the next two hours. His was the only car left except for a government car parked in front of it. The bishops too were the only people left except for soldiers and military police. They had been there since nine in the morning and it was now nearly five.

Bishop Wani asked a soldier what was delaying the Archbishop. 'He is still in serious discussion with the President,' he was told. In fact Luwum had been hustled into a car and was already on his way to the State Research headquarters at Nakasero. At the same time Oryema and Oboth-Ofumbi had been arrested on the other side of the Conference Centre by secret police who had been waiting for them.

Bishop Wani was not satisfied and eventually managed to speak to the Chief of Staff of the Armed Forces, who also said that he thought the Archbishop was still talking with either the President or the Vice-President in the Nile Hotel. After a short while they approached the soldiers guarding the Nile Hotel and asked why the Archbishop was not coming out. 'You go home,' said the guards. 'We will bring him in another car.' The bishops stayed firm. 'We came with him; it would be embarrassing to go without him.' Their stand was to no avail. They had an argument with the security men and one of the officers came up and said, 'This is an order! Get in your car and go!' The bishops replied that they had no intention of going without their Archbishop and the officers asked them, 'Don't you think that we too are God's people?' 'We don't know, we hope so,' they answered. Two military policemen then came and forced them at gunpoint into the car and made them drive away. As they sat in the car Bishop Wani shouted, 'I hope you will bring our Archbishop.' 'Yes, sir,' said the policemen.

At the Archbishop's house they rejoined the other bishops and held prayers. Then Mary Luwum and the provincial secretary returned with Bishop Wani and Bishop Kivengere in the Archbishop's car to the Conference Centre. 'I must see if I can do something,' said Mary. 'Perhaps they will allow me to see my husband.' She was repulsed by the guards at the gate. Forlornly, the four returned home. At 6.30 Radio Uganda announced that the Archbishop and the two cabinet ministers had been arrested pending further investigations. The night was long and fearful and in the wait of the dawn the Archbishop's family and brother bishops prayed for his safe keeping.

Early the next morning they sat in his office discussing what they should do about his arrest, when news of his death was announced both on the radio and in the state-owned newspaper, *Voice of Uganda*. The Archbishop and the two ministers had died in a road accident on their way from the Nile Hotel to the Interrogation Centre of the State Research Bureau a quarter of a mile away. This was the official story and it was incredible.

Bishop Kivengere went with two other bishops to the hospital to claim the Archbishop's body so that they could prepare for the funeral. Many of the nurses and doctors were in tears. 'We want to see the superintendent,' urged the bishops, but they could speak only to his assistant who was signing a document. His hand was trembling and there was a security man at his back. The bishops waited for more than an hour and were eventually taken to the mortuary.

What had happened there was later described by Henry Kyemba after he had defected to Britain. 'When an army lorry brought the bullet-riddled bodies of Archbishop Luwum and the two ministers to the mortuary, they were simply thrown out of the back of the truck like sacks of coffee. It was dreadful. The Archbishop was still in his robes, with a cross on a chain around his neck.'

Kyemba had been informed of the 'motor accident' in a telephone call from the Vice-President, Mustafa Adrisi, at 9.00 p.m. the previous night. He said he was calling on Amin's orders. Amin himself then added a phrase which he also used in giving the news to his Minister of Justice, Godfrey Lule, 'God has given them their punishment.' Kyemba *knew* the three men had been killed. The story was fantastic. He could not believe that they had died accidentally so soon after their accusation when they had left the proceedings in two different cars. Kyemba alerted Mulago mortuary to expect the bodies, which eventually arrived at about 5.00 a.m.

The mortuary had been guarded by armed sentries since 6 p.m.

the previous evening. The bishops were not allowed in; but through the gates they saw some nurses washing blood from one of the corridors. They were ordered away.

Later that day evidence from three eye-witnesses reached the bishops that their Primate had been shot dead. A nurse who worked at the hospital told them she had seen the Archbishop's body with two bullet holes in his chest and blood in his mouth. Shooting victims in the mouth had characterized recent killings in Uganda; it was the tyrant's way of stopping an argument, or silencing an Archbishop who said his prayers aloud. Amin's former doctor, John Kibukamusoke, who had fled Uganda four years before to save his life, told a British newspaper (*The Observer*) that according to his information Luwum had been shot in the mouth by Amin while praying aloud in defiance of orders. The President had been trying to get the Archbishop to sign a confession about his alleged part in the attempted coup. He refused and started praying. 'Confronted with this kind of defiance it is reasonable to expect that a person suffering from hypomania would "shut him up" by shooting him in the mouth.'

In the afternoon the bishops went to the Minister of Health to ask for the body; but their appeals were unheeded. When they returned to the Provincial Office a Christian soldier was waiting to tell them that he had seen the Archbishop and the ministers shot and then a vehicle run over their bodies. An hour later corroboration came from a doctor at the hospital who had managed to see the bullet-ridden bodies while the guards were being changed.

News sources gave confused and contradictory accounts of the 'motor accident'. Henry Kyemba, however, has since revealed that he was telephoned by Amin the next day because he wanted a 'medical cover-up' for Major Moses Okello, the driver of one vehicle, who claimed he did not remember the accident because he was knocked unconscious and was in a coma for two days. Amin was anxious that Moses should have a hospital 'examination' to substantiate his claim. Later Amin was asked by a foreign TV crew about the other driver. He replied that he had been knocked out too. But it was outrageous even for Amin to insist that both drivers had been knocked unconscious and were totally ignorant of what had happened, so a new 'official story' now described one car as stationary and driverless.

Pictures were released of the two vehicles involved in the 'crash': one a Range Rover (UVW 082) which was the President's personal car and had been damaged at some time in a smash; the other was a Toyota (UVS 299), one of the State Research Bureau's fleet which had also been in a crash and was in the State Research garage for a couple of weeks before the incident.

The bishops went on pleading with the Government to release the body for the funeral service but to no avail. Amin instructed the Army to make arrangements for the burials, without telling his Health Minister or any of the relatives. Meanwhile the bodies of all three men were driven to Army headquarters and kept in one of the barracks.

Some time during the next week, the body of Janani was sent to his home village near Kitgum in the north and buried without ceremony, watched over by soldiers. Some Christians, who fled into Kenya, saw it, naked, mutilated, with his cassock beside him in the coffin. Oryema was buried near Gulu and Oboth-Ofumbi near Torono. When Henry Kyemba left Uganda for Britain two and a half months later all three graves were still under guard by Amin's Army.

*

At the headquarters of the Church Missionary Society in London's Waterloo Road, the 'phones were busy. The news media were seeking 'background' for their stories, the biographical details of the martyred Archbishop, who was a world-renowned figure.

Born at Mucwini in 1924, he went to school in Kitgum, the administrative centre of East Acholi. It was an Englishwoman, a C.M.S. missionary, Phebe Cave-Browne-Cave, now over eighty and still working in Gulu in the north, who first encouraged a keen young pupil at school and helped him, first to become a teacher, then a lay reader, and later a priest. He did not get secondary education but became an unlicensed teacher in a 'sub-grade' school, and from his small salary saved enough to support himself when he entered a teacher-training college for vernacular teachers, the lowest category of college.

He discovered his vocation while studying, and in 1949 was accepted on the first lay readers' course conducted in English at what was then the theological college of his diocese at Buwalasi.

At the end of 1950 he was attached to St. Philip's Church in Gulu as a lay reader and he also taught the catechists at the arch-deaconry training centre. He was then accepted for a further three-year course at Buwalasi leading to ordination by Bishop Keith Russell in Northern Uganda in 1955. In 1958 Luwum first came to England and studied for a year at St. Augustine's College, Canterbury. On his return he became pastor at Lira-Palwo in East Acholi and rural dean. Then, in 1962, the year of Uganda's Inde-pendence, he joined the staff of his old college at Buwalasi as vice-principal.

The C.M.S. could find plenty of material for the press including tribute from his holiday hostess in this country. When Janani Luwum returned to England in 1963 to continue his studies at St. John's College, Northwood, London (then the London College of Divinity and now St. John's College, Nottingham) he spent his vacations with Neville Sugden, vicar of St. Mary's, Shortlands, Bromley in Kent, and his wife, Joan, whom he had met five years earlier when at Canterbury. Bishop Keith Russell had preached at St. Mary's, Shortlands, in 1963 and mentioned in his sermon that the African Church had 'an outstanding priest'. They wanted to train him at an English University and needed money for his travelling expenses. The parish collected enough to pay the air fares and to bring Mary to join Janani in London for three months so that she could be trained to help him in his future position.

At the Kent vicarage Janani entered fully into the activities of a busy parish and the family life of the household where there were four young children. In the parish magazine of St. Peter's Church, Harrogate (March 1977), the new living of the Sugdens, Joan re-called how 'this gentle giant of a man would stand often waving a tea-towel in the kitchen – "Come along, Mother, and we'll help with the drying up".' He would burn the midnight oil studying Hebrew and Greek and there was never a word of self-pity at the long hours he needed to work.

It was no surprise to them when he went home to become Principal at Buwalasi, and then Provincial Secretary of the Church of Uganda, experience which was to stand him in good stead as he climbed the leadership ladder. In 1968 he was one of the Arch-bishop of Canterbury's consultants at the Lambeth Conference and soon afterwards he was elected Bishop of Northern Uganda.

In 1974 the House of Bishops chose him as Archbishop and Metro-politan of the Province of Uganda, Rwanda and Boga-Zaire, to succeed Erica Sabiti and become the second African Archbishop.

Dr. Leslie Brown, Bishop of St. Edmondsbury and Ipswich, who had been the first Archbishop of Uganda and the last white Arch-bishop, paid homage in the *Church Times*. 'Those who knew him best are sure he was guilty of no crime against the State. Rather he was a devoted lover of Uganda and protested openly and char-itably against abuses which besmirched his country's good name and brought fear and insecurity to the population.' He was 'a big man in body and spirit, his judgments were mature and his de-votion very evident.'

Sylvia Rice-Oxley, the Archbishop's personal secretary for 18 months, now back in London at C.M.S. headquarters, was much in demand by television, radio and press. She was asked if the Arch-bishop ever appeared to be frightened of what might happen to him. 'Well, he was human,' she said. 'So I suppose that he did have fear within him for what might eventually happen. But that didn't matter. He was standing up for what was right and what he felt Jesus would stand up for and so he did it fearlessly.'

Canon W. H. A. Butler, then general secretary of the Rwanda Mission, also went on ITN to talk about what was obviously a trumped-up charge. 'He was a man of immense courage and integ-rity and totally loyal to the Government in all that pertained to the country's good.'

The three men died in Kampala on the very day when the Gen-eral Synod of the Church of England in London was proclaiming the importance of human rights. The sitting of the Synod was interrupted to announce the death of the Archbishop and Dr. Donald Coggan, Archbishop of Canterbury, spoke of 'the great courage and gentleness of my friend'. It was inconceivable he had been involved in a plot – 'I know my Archbishop.'

*

On a cold spring evening in London on the last day of March, as the dusk dropped a grey veil over the massive outlines of West-minster Abbey, people gathered to remember the witness of Janani Luwum, bishop, pastor, patriot. The worshippers were of all ages, black and white, of every denomination. There were bishops in rich robes, Government representatives from many nations in sombre suits, teenagers in their jeans, young mothers and vociferous children, the famous and the unknown.

The Dean of Westminster, Dr. Edward Carpenter, standing at the high altar, said, 'We meet to commemorate and to celebrate the true self-giving of our beloved friend, Janani Luwum. We give thanks that he was raised up to be a witness to the triumph of love.'

His words set the theme for a service impressive for its staunch happiness. The beautiful familiar reassurance of the 23rd Psalm, 'The Lord's my Shepherd, I'll not want,' was followed by the account of the undaunted witness of the early Church.

The Rev. Harry Morton, General Secretary of the British Council of Churches, read from Hebrews, Chapter XI.

What shall I more say? For the time would fail me to tell of Gideon and of Barak, and of Samson, and of Jephthae; of David also, and Samuel, and of the prophets: who through faith subdued kingdoms, wrought righteousness, obtained promises, stopped the mouths of lions, quenched the violence of fire, escaped the edge of the sword, out of weakness were made strong, waxed valiant in fight, turned to flight the armies of the aliens . . .

The words challenged the congregation.

Wherefore seeing we also are compassed about with so great a cloud of witnesses, let us lay aside every weight, and the sin which doth so easily beset us, and let us run with patience the race that is set before us, looking unto Jesus the author and finisher of our faith.

Bishop Keith Russell, Assistant Bishop of Rochester and formerly Bishop of Northern Uganda, read the second lesson, the hard requirement from St. Matthew, 'If any man will come after me, let him deny himself, and take up his cross and follow me.'

Later the hymn 'For all the saints who from their labours rest' acclaimed the martyred Archbishop.

Sylvia Rice-Oxley heard the rustling of the people for offerings to the Archbishop Luwum Memorial Fund. She knew how much her former boss would approve of its educational aims: to allow more priests of the Church of Uganda to study at St. John's College, more Church leaders to travel, more books to be bought. Students from the U.K. too would be encouraged to spend part of their training in Uganda. Sylvia saw in her mind's eye the powerful figure of the Archbishop as he stood in African pulpits exhorting the people to give only their best to God. He used to say, 'Would you give a visitor to your house the parson's nose, or the breast of the chicken? Would you dig deep into your pockets' — here he would forage cheerfully under the many folds of his robes — 'past all the paper money to find your smallest coin to give for God?'

For Bishop Leslie Brown, who gave the address, it was the second commemorative service he had attended for Janani Luwum. The day after the Archbishop's death he had flown to Africa to represent the Church of England, the Archbishop of Canterbury, and the Anglican Consultative Council. He found the frontiers of Uganda closed and both the funeral and memorial services in Kampala cancelled.

Instead Dr. Brown spoke at a packed service in Nairobi Cathedral. Hundreds more stood outside to hear him declare, 'We shall be strengthened by his martyrdom just as we have been through the years by the memory of the first Ugandan martyrs.'

Now before an assembly of the august and the humble in Westminster Abbey he outlined the events which had led to the Archbishop's death and said, 'Maybe there is no answer to evil except the self-sacrifice of Christ and those who will die with him.' He went on, 'I believe that the Archbishop and his brother bishops in pleading for peace and compassion in Uganda were appealing for the right of human beings to live without fear and in security.' He saluted the first martyr of the second century of the Church of Uganda, who had shouldered his cross and given his life for God and nation.

Helmuth James von Moltke

1907–1945

Like Luwum, Helmuth von Moltke, international lawyer and land-owner, felt compelled to oppose a godless rule. He chose as a German Christian to fight the Nazi menace from within, indeed from the very centre of 'the nest of vipers'. Moltke felt that it was his duty to do more than console or bury those run over by a madman; he had to get out into the middle of the road and try to stop the car; but he was not prepared to shoot the driver. His religious scruples forbade him to connive in the plot on Hitler's life.

Many Christian opponents of Nazism were also politically motivated and power-conscious. They wanted to preserve the privilege of the Church, and self-interest was sometimes para-mount. With Helmuth it was his faith in God which was the mainspring of his resistance. It was Moltke's greatest victory at his trial that his prosecutors cried out in utter vexation, 'The trouble with you is that you are a Christian!'

The People's Court in Berlin in 1945 had to move from place to place because of air attacks by the Allies, and the small hall on the Bellevue Strasse, which resembled a schoolroom, was crammed. The air inside seemed dense with suspicions and secrets, and the stormy scene in the building commandeered for the trial was dominated by the defendant, tall of stature and of aristocratic demeanour. Someone had once said of Helmuth James von Moltke, 'He personified grace under pressure.' Now he stood in the dock. He was thirty-eight years old, six feet seven inches tall, dressed in sombre suit, white shirt and habitual black tie. He had been heartily glad to exchange the blue and white striped pyjamas worn by inmates of concentration camps for his tailored Viennese suit.

Slowly a smile spread over his serious impressive face. The judge, Roland Freisler, a Russian prisoner-of-war in the first world war who had traded Communism for Nazism, had been goaded to reveal his hand, and that of his implacable masters of the Third

Reich. In the course of one of his tirades he declared, 'Graf Moltke, Christianity and we National Socialists have one thing in common and one thing only: we claim the whole man.' He glanced at the Führer's picture on the wall as if for commendation.

It was with a sense of extraordinary triumph that Helmuth von Moltke, great-grand-nephew of the famous Field Marshal of Bismarck's era, heard these words which he described in a jubilant letter to his beloved wife, Freya, as 'the decisive phrase in the proceedings'. In that instant he realized he was to be convicted 'not as a Protestant, not as a landowner, not as a noble, not as a Prussian, not as a German even, but *as a Christian* and nothing else. The prosecution had made clear that Moltke was opposed in principle to large estates, and he had no class interests at heart. In fact, he had no personal interests at all; not even those of his wartime job in the Supreme Command, 'but he stood for the cause of all mankind'. Helmuth was moved to write in awe to his wife, 'that I should have been chosen to undertake so mighty a task!'

Helmuth was the eldest of five Moltke children, four boys and a girl, who inherited traditions of efficiency and public service, and of ideas of liberty and justice for the oppressed. Their English mother, Countess Dorothy, was the daughter of James and Jessie Rose Innes who were South Africans. James Rose Innes, also a jurist, was made Chief Justice of the Transvaal by Lord Milner. Helmuth became unusually fond of his grandparents. Sir James's rational outlook and unshakeable sense of justice impressed him enormously, and Helmuth's mother, who was imbued with high ideals, was undoubtedly the major influence in his life. His father was a landowner, who inherited the beautiful thousand-acre estate of Kreisau, near Schweidnitz in Silesia.

Their home at Kreisau had been in the family since the old Field Marshal of Bismarck's time bought it with the rewards (£30,000) for his military services. As a further accolade he was made a count in 1871. (All titles were abolished in Germany in 1919 and Freya is emphatic that Helmuth should not be called count or herself countess). But the funds of the family trust the Field Marshal founded to maintain the estate were wiped out by inflation after the first world war, and in 1930 creditors put in an inspector to administer it. It was Helmuth's acumen and industry which reclaimed it for the Moltkes. After five years all debts were discharged and the inspector stayed on as Moltke's employee.

Helmuth interpreted his role of landowner as one of responsibilities rather than of rights and showed genuine concern for everyone living on the estate which he now began to run on a profit-sharing basis. But much as he loved the country he did not want to spend his life farming and decided to study law with politics his goal.

From the first Helmuth took a serious view of the threat of the National Socialist Party and he regarded Hitler's accession to power in 1933 as a catastrophe of the first magnitude. He said from the start, 'Voting for Hitler means voting for war.'

He continued with his legal training through 1933, although the Nazis brought in regulations which closed his prospects of a judicial career. He began to practise as an international lawyer in Berlin and in the next six years Helmuth gave priority to helping Jews and other anti-Nazis who wished to leave Germany. On one occasion two of his clients vanished and he took his inquiries to the Gestapo headquarters in Vienna, ignoring those who warned him that if he put his head in the lion's mouth he too might disappear.

Helmuth became so depressed by the atmosphere of the Third Reich that to get some relief from it he arranged to be called to the English Bar, since the need to attend dinners would allow for frequent visits to London. Among the first people he sought out was Lionel Curtis, Oxford don, Fellow of All Souls, and a friend of his grandparents in South Africa. Lionel Curtis introduced him to a wide and influential circle of people and Helmuth was frequently in England until the summer of 1939 when he qualified for the English Bar.

More than once he thought about practising as an international lawyer in Britain, his time divided between London and Kreisau. He told Lionel Curtis at this time, 'What really attracts me is not this vague gambling chance at the Bar but the possibility that I might be useful in defending and perhaps restating the European creed versus the Caesarian: in short the attraction really lies in being on the right side.'

Freya viewed with apparent equanimity Helmuth's suggestion made just before the Munich crisis, that she should cut herself sufficiently loose from the Kreisau household to train in agriculture. This, he argued, would mean she could then support herself and the children if he were to leave Germany. He once asserted that he had more friends in London than Berlin, and among the godfathers of his two sons were two Englishmen.

However, September 1939 found Helmuth based in Berlin, with the Foreign Countries Division of the Abwehr (the Military Intelligence Department) in the Supreme Command of the Armed Forces (OKW). He advised on international law and economic warfare and in the course of his work evaluated much secret intelligence material. The job suited his purposes admirably. It gave him official justification for keeping in touch with countries outside Germany, particularly Britain – he read *The Times* and *Hansard* throughout the war – and he could visit neutral countries. It also gave him a chance to ensure that Germany at war observed the rules of international law, and when he could not flout or circumvent official orders he strove to mitigate their inhumanity. Although he never wore uniform he became a member of the Armed Forces and so claimed, theoretically anyway, their protection against the Nazi party. The personal file of anyone working for the Abwehr was transferred to its records from those of the police.

Although Helmuth judged correctly that the best chance of organizing opposition to the Third Reich was from inside, he did not suspect that he was, in fact, entering the nerve-centre of machinations to overthrow Hitler.

There were inside the High Command several groups of officers who had begun as early as 1938 to plan to bring down the Nazi régime. The army opposition concentrated around Colonel-General Ludwig Beck, then Chief of the Army General Staff, and found support from Ernst Weizsäcker, State Secretary, and other Foreign Office officials. An alternative post-war civil régime was planned under the aegis of Karl Goerdeler, whose disapproval of Nazism led him to relinquish his post as Commissar for Price Control, just as his hatred of anti-Semitism made him resign the office of Lord Mayor of Leipzig. Beck was to be Head of State and Goerdeler Shadow Chancellor.

In the group that formed around Helmuth, the 'Kreisau circle', the main object was to prepare for the sequel to Hitler's fall and to plan for the rebirth of a democratic Germany. The paramount task was to make crystal clear the crucial issues involved; if the war were to be lost by internal German revolt these issues could be obscured. The Widerstand (Resistance), Helmuth believed, were not so much in conflict with a régime as with a perversion of the human spirit which might even survive in defeat. He saw Nazism as a virus invading the German bloodstream and bringing consequences far beyond vainglorious militarism. Helmuth believed Goerdeler to be sincere in wanting a new start for Germany but too intransigent in his ideas to realize what this meant. Towards the end, because he was indiscreet, Goerdeler began to be regarded as a security risk and there was a move to replace him as Shadow Chancellor.

There was also the 'Group of Counts', friends of Peter Yorck von Wartenburg, who, like Helmuth, was descended from a distinguished figure in German military history (Field Marshal Hans David Ludwig Yorck von Wartenburg in 1812 began the campaign which led to the Battle of Leipzig and the overthrow of Napoleon). Peter studied law, and was also a big landowner. He became a civil servant, working in the Price Control Office, although in August 1939 he was called up as a reserve lieutenant and served in the Polish campaign. He became an intermediary between Helmuth's circle and the counts, most of whom regarded Helmuth as disloyal to his class, because he opposed inequality and privilege, and to his country, for openly proposing a federated Germany within a federated Europe. Weekend gatherings were held not only at Kreisau but at the estates of Peter Yorck, and meetings went on incessantly in Berlin and sometimes in Munich.

All these groups were informal and without any definite membership. They had their agreements and differences over policies. Nobody connected with the Kreisau circle ever used the name. That was coined by the Security Service, who liked a label, when they made their inquiries after the July 20 plot. Helmuth's type of resistance differed fundamentally from those who thought in traditional terms of a coup, but he had periods of vacillation about killing Hitler.

At first, both as a statesman and as a Christian he opposed plans to assassinate the Führer. He said to Hans Christoph Stauffenberg early in 1943, 'Why are we opposed to the Third Reich and to National Socialism? Surely because it is a criminal system and one ought not to begin something new with a new crime. Murder is always a crime.' That was his platform. He objected to behaving in the very way for which the Nazis were denounced.

Nevertheless, his awareness of the continual suffering went deep. 'How can one bear one's share of guilt?' he wrote to Freya. 'How can one know things like this and yet walk about a free man? If only I could be rid of the awful feeling that I have let myself be corrupted, that I no longer react keenly enough to such things.' Helmuth was haunted by feelings of complicity and impotence, and in the spring of 1943 he asked Einvind Berggrav, Bishop of Oslo, and prime mover in the Norwegian Resistance, if it would be right for a Christian to kill Hitler. His self-appointed role was to plan for a new government; but if Hitler could not be disposed of without him, he was ready to play his part. Berggrav said it was the most difficult question ever put to him. He believed that in certain circumstances the killing of a tyrant could be justified, but it was already too late to kill Hitler. Those contemplating such an act ought to be able to assassinate him and to form a new government which could secure peace, but the war had reached a stage when any new German government could no longer do this.

By the summer of the same year Helmuth seemed to have resolved any doubts. He told Dr. Gottfried von Falkenhausen, a civil servant attached to the German Embassy in Paris, 'Let him (Hitler) live. He and his party must shoulder right to the end the responsibility for the terrible fate which they have brought on the German people. This is the only way to eradicate the ideology of National Socialism.' Yet the autumn brought another bout of irresolution and he told this man's uncle, General Alexander von Falkenhausen, Military Commander, Belgium, 'Despite all doubts we have no other choice open to us except to eliminate Hitler physically.'

This was but a transient change of heart, and in a last letter to his young sons he reiterated his early condemnation of violence. 'I never wished for or contributed to acts of violence like that of 20 July [Colonel Klaus von Stauffenberg's unsuccessful attempt with a bomb which he planted under a table in the Führer's military headquarters at Rastenburg] but fought preparations for them because I disapproved on many grounds, and, above all, believed they would not get rid of the fundamental trouble which was spiritual.' He even told Freya, when she went to see him in prison, 'If I had been at liberty, this wouldn't have happened.'

*

Although he was not prepared to kill Hitler, Moltke and others of his circle managed to throw quite a lot of grit into the Nazi machine. Helmuth intervened with some effect to stop the illegal shootings and deportations of hostages by Nazis in occupied countries who were ruthless in their measures to counter opposition. An occupying power which encountered resistance was entitled by international law to take hostages provided they were not treated as convicts. The Nazis tried to prevent resistance by punishing and shooting; but this policy often had the opposite effect. Helmuth worked to get the practice abandoned as militarily ineffective, and he did not pull any punches.

He wrote to Freya in June 1943, 'I was called on to advise the murderous group of officers in the OKW [High Command] who hang on the Führer's every word, and I put them one and all to flight by vigorous attacks. They called my attention to the fact that what I wanted conflicted with a directive of the Führer. I answered, "But gentlemen, you can't creep to shelter behind a directive of the Führer's. We would be failing flagrantly in our duty to the Führer if we were too cowardly to say to him that he was wrongly advised, and if, as a result of our cowardice, our troops away on service were to lose their lives." That was roughly the line with which I jumped on these filthy toadies and, although one or two got indignant, they all turned tail in the end.'

Another cause for his concern was the treatment of nationals of countries like Poland, France and Yugoslavia, whose governments had surrendered to Germany. What was the status of those who had joined the 'free' forces fighting with the Allies if they were captured? A similar problem arose with Allied personnel fighting with Resistance forces, whom the Nazis would shoot on capture. Helmuth sought to find grounds in international law for giving both groups some protection. He was one of those who warned the Danish Jews of plans to send them to the Eastern death camps. He tried to alert Polish villages that the SS intended to surround them by night and seize all the men as hostages against further acts by the Polish Resistance. A caution from him also saved the life on one occasion of the Norwegian Bishop Berggrav.

It was humanitarian work by Helmuth, working at the operational centre of the secret service, which first led to his arrest. In January 1944 he warned a man who was wanted by the Gestapo. This man was captured and under pressure gave information which betrayed Helmuth.

It was after his arrest that the officers in the Abwehr became more insistent in urging that Hitler be assassinated, and they converted some members of the Kreisau group to this outlook. Peter Yorck, a cousin of Stauffenberg who placed the bomb, was won over in the end to the argument that the July 20 attempt was essential to demonstrate to the world the existence of 'another Germany'. One of those involved in the OKW building which was the headquarters of the plot, he was arrested, and tried with seven other officers on 8 August 1944. All were executed.

*

Freisler, bullying, ruthless, nervous, glory-seeking, seemed more suited to the stage than a court. Hercher, defence counsel, described him as 'talented, with some genius in him, and unintelligent, and all three in the highest degree'; and Helmuth endorsed this as accurate.

Twice the trial had been postponed. The authorities had not found it easy to indict Helmuth who had been in prison for six months at the time of the assassination attempt, although they had found documents incriminating a number of members of the Kreisau circle. They were probably determined to kill him, irrespective of the difficulties in finding justification, because they sensed that Helmuth personified many of the high-principled and Christian influences which had stood between them and success. Others tried alongside Helmuth on January 9 and 10 1945 had been more politically active, even closely involved in the plot of July 20. Yet it was Moltke who became the central figure in the court. He wrote to Freya, 'My name was brought in by Freisler in every other sentence ... "the Moltke circle" ... "Moltke's plans" ... "also belonging to Moltke" ...' It ran like a scarlet thread through all the cross-examinations.

On the first day the People's Court reminded the defendants of 'fundamental principles of the law'. The Court regarded failure to report defeatist utterances as treasonable, especially when emanating from a man of Moltke's consequence and position. It was also 'tantamount to preparation for high treason' to broach matters of high policy with people who were in no way competent to deal with them, particularly when they did not belong to the Party. The same view was taken of anyone who presumed to form an opinion about a matter that it was the Führer's business to decide. Again it was considered as preparation for high treason for anyone, 'even while himself holding aloof from all violent action, to plan measures for the event when a third party, namely the enemy, shall have overthrown the Government by force, for by so doing he is counting on the force of the enemy.'

Helmuth observed laconically, and a lot more succinctly to Freya, 'It is tantamount to high treason if one does not suit Herr Freisler.'

The first of the five to be tried that day was the young Jesuit father and sociologist Alfred Delp. He was introduced to the Kreisau circle by Helmuth in 1942, for he gathered around him people not so much like-minded and congenial to him as those with the expertise needed to rebuild a democratic Germany. For this task Helmuth saw the mobilization of the Church as of paramount importance.

Insults now assailed the Catholic clergy and the Jesuits. Even the absence of Delp from the discussions held at his quarters was denigrated as 'typically Jesuitical'. Freisler bawled at him, 'By that very action you yourself showed that you knew perfectly well that high treason was afoot, out of which such a holy consecrated fellow would naturally be only too anxious to keep his tonsured pate. So off he goes to church, to pray the while, that the plot may develop along lines pleasing to God.'

Helmuth's turn came on the second day, 10 January. Freisler had no compunction about combining the role of judge with that of prosecutor. He started off mildly but at breakneck speed. Helmuth wrote to Freya, ' 'It was a sort of dialogue of the spirit between Freisler and me. Freisler was the only one of the whole gang who thoroughly understood me, and the only one who realized why he must do away with me.'

The first uproar in court, or, as Helmuth termed it, 'Freisler's paroxysm No. 1,' came when he interrupted to object that the police and the security authorities had known all about his conversations with Goerdeler, the former Commissar for Price Control.

At Helmuth's interruption Freisler banged on the table, went as red as his robe, and bellowed, 'I won't stand that; I won't listen to that sort of thing.'

Helmuth described the court scene to Freya. 'Everything that Delp had experienced was child's play by comparison. A hurricane was let loose ... I looked Freisler icily straight in the eye and suddenly could not keep myself from smiling.' He had a keen sense of the ludicrous and bogus. His smile shocked the onlookers as well as the official public prosecutor, Schulze. 'I wish you could have seen Schulze's expression,' wrote Helmuth. And he added with impish humour, 'If a man were to jump off the bridge over the crocodiles' pond at the Zoo, I don't think the uproar could be greater!'

As order returned, Freisler wasted no time in emphasizing the central charges against Helmuth – defeatism, and the selection of Land Commissioners, who, for an interim period after a collapse of the régime, were intended to take over in each part of Germany with plenary powers.

Helmuth reported to Freya, 'Both gave rise to fresh paroxysms as violent as before, and, when I submitted in defence that it all had come about as an offshoot of my official duties, a third paroxysm was provoked. Freisler bellowed, "All Adolf Hitler's officials set about their work on the assumption of victory, and that applies just as much in the High Command as anywhere else. It's clearly the duty of every single man for his own part to promote confidence in victory." '

Next Freisler turned to Moltke's overtures to the Church. In the autumn of 1941 Father Augustin Rösch, head of the Jesuit Province of Munich, was drawn into the group. The following year Helmuth had approached Bishop Theophilus Wurm of Württemberg, one of the pastors who initiated the 'Confessing Church' of Christians not prepared to accept the faithless compromises proposed by the men Hitler put at the head of the Protestant Church. His talks with the Bishop first brought Helmuth into contact with Dr. Eugen Gerstenmaier, whom he called 'Wurm's man in Berlin'. Gerstenmaier worked in the Church Office for External Affairs and held a post in the Information Department of the Foreign Office. He became one of Helmuth's closest collaborators. In the spring of 1943 Helmuth wrote to Lionel Curtis in England via Swedish friends, 'The whole clergy, practically without exception, have upheld the great principles in spite of all the intense propaganda and pressure exerted against them.' Some of the sermons of the more prominent bishops which denounced Nazi conduct became known abroad.

Now Moltke's Church 'contacts' came in for Freisler's abuse. 'And who was present at these discussions? A Jesuit father! And with him of all people, you discuss civil disobedience. And a Protestant minister, and three others who were later condemned to death for complicity in the July 20 plot! And not a single National Socialist! And the Provincial Head of the Jesuits, you know him too! He even came to Kreisau once! And you're not ashamed of it, even though no decent German would touch a Jesuit with a barge-pole! People who have been excluded from all military service because of their attitude! ... And you went visiting bishops! Looking for something you'd lost I suppose? From whom do you take your orders? From the other world or from Adolf Hitler? Where lies your loyalty and your faith?' 'Rhetorical questions of course', Helmuth observed to Freya.

Rhetorical perhaps, but Freisler had indeed gone to the heart of the matter. Helmuth had written to Freya on 3 November 1942, 'Bürkner [his boss, Rear-Admiral Leopold Bürkner] was reluctant to sign something to which I attached great importance and argued with me about the justification for an absolutely murderous order of the Führer's. I said to him, "Look here, Admiral, the difference between us is that I am incapable of arguing about such things. So long as orders exist for me which no order of the Führer's can annul, and which have to be acted on even in the face of an order from the Führer, I can't allow such things to pass because the difference between good and evil, right and wrong, is fixed for me from the very outset. That's got nothing to do with the expediency of the arguments." Whereupon he signed without hesitation. I was interested to see once again how such people can be got on to the right side if only one takes up a resolute attitude.'

*

It was not revealed at the trial how much the prosecution knew about the 'house-parties' at Kreisau, which were the 'cover' for meetings of Helmuth's fellow-conspirators to discuss a new Germany born out of defeat. Helmuth had prepared summaries of conclusions for those too prominent or too suspect to attend.

The first meeting in the spring of 1942 discussed the proper relationship between Church and state. Then, since the Churches were so much involved with education, they had debated the whole question of Church schools and educational reform. This was politically the most innocent of their topics and so if they had underestimated the chances of secrecy, the consequences would be the least serious for them.

Helmuth, and most of his confederates, wanted to restore religion to the heart of German life but as a unifying force and no longer a divisive one. All schools should have Christian instruction but were to be interdenominational (which primary schools were not before the war). Another progressive idea was the proposed Una Sancta, a German, and indeed a world-wide, Christian community, to which all Christians could belong regardless of their confession. The main role of Una Sancta would be to ensure that the Christian standpoint got a full hearing in political and social discussions.

After the first meeting Helmuth personally assumed the task of informing Church leaders of 'results'. He visited the Bishop of Berlin, Count Konrad von Preysing, one of the most implacable opponents of the Nazis among the Catholic hierarchy. The Bishop was sympathetic but not prepared to take the lead in pressing these ideas on his fellow bishops. The Jesuit, Father Rösch from Munich, contacted Cardinal Michael von Faulhaber, also of Munich, whose reaction was similar. Archbishop Konrad Gröber of Freiburg and Bishop Johannes Dietz of Fulda were also disinclined to help.

The experience of the Kreisau circle in resisting evil had convinced them that a humanist benevolence was inadequate. It had been a personal revelation to Helmuth. He wrote an explanation to Lionel Curtis in England (the letter was written on a visit to Sweden and reached London in June 1942 through the Special Operations Executive). 'Perhaps you will remember that in discussions before the war I maintained that belief in God was not essential for coming to the results you arrive at. Today I know I was wrong, completely wrong. You know that I have fought the Nazis from the first day but the amount of risk and readiness for sacrifice which is asked from us now, and that which may be asked tomorrow, require *more* than right ethical principles.'

Around this time two memoranda reached the British. They were not Kreisau documents but prepared by people who were, or became, Helmuth's close collaborators. One was brought to London by Dr. Willem Visser 't Hooft, general secretary of the Provisional Committee of what was to become in 1948 the World Council of Churches. The other was handed to the English Bishop, George Bell of Chichester, in Stockholm by Dr. Hans Schönfeld, a Lutheran pastor and research director of the Provisional Committee, at a meeting also attended by Dietrich Bonhoeffer. Both documents argued in favour of a negotiated peace between the new German régime and the British and Americans after the overthrow of Hitler. Both Bonhoeffer and Moltke were convinced Christians and inexorable opponents of Hitler but they never became close friends. In April 1942 they made a trip to Scandinavia together on behalf of the Abwehr. Quisling, on becoming Prime Minister of Norway, had precipitated a row with the Church over the control of youth and forbidden the Provost of Trondheim Cathedral to hold services. This had resulted in the Norwegian bishops and then the pastors laying down their offices. Quisling arrested Berggrav, Bishop of Oslo, on Easter Sunday. (He was imprisoned and then transferred to house-arrest at his home although the guards lent him a policeman's uniform any time he wanted to go into the city!) Moltke and Bonhoeffer had their instructions to point out to the civilian authorities that if all Norway was stirred into unrest, German troops badly needed elsewhere would be tied down in the country. They were also told to encourage the Norwegians against giving way and Helmuth took the opportunity to tell them about the work which he had organized in Germany.

It is unlikely that Moltke and Bonhoeffer met again. They disagreed on whether a Christian might work for the assassination of Hitler, and Helmuth was likely to have felt uncomfortable in Bonhoeffer's abstract theological discussions. Helmuth had his own satisfactory contacts with the Protestant Churches, some of whom were opposed to Bonhoeffer. It may also have been feared that Bonhoeffer's attendance at discussions of Moltke's group would attract suspicion. Bonhoeffer was already a marked man, employed in the Abwehr because he was forbidden either to preach or teach. (He was arrested in the spring of 1943 and hanged at Flossenburg on 9 April 1945.)

In March 1943 Moltke took the plunge and in a long letter to Lionel Curtis asked for British help in their internal war against Hitler. He wanted a man in Stockholm to keep in touch with the European 'underground' but free of all entanglements of secret service work. The request was not met. Churchill had directed that any approaches from Germans were to be disregarded. Roosevelt too, in 1944, after Helmuth was gaoled, firmly refused to treat with 'those East German Junkers'. Yet another approach was believed to have been made by Helmuth and his friends to the U.S. Naval Attaché in Turkey, who told them to direct such proposals to General Eisenhower. The failure to establish contact with the West made those who came to Kreisau in Whitsun 1943 favour sounding out Russian reaction in the hope that they might consider peace on terms more liberal than unconditional surrender. There is no doubt they tried, but there is no evidence of any success.

The second weekend gathering at Kreisau in the previous autumn (1942) debated the organization of the state and the economy. The following Whitsun saw the third and last meeting there when more dangerous ground was covered. Firstly, post-war foreign policy. Second, the trial and punishment of German war criminals not by a tribunal of victors, but by the International Court of Justice at the Hague. And thirdly, the instructions to Land Commissioners. Both the Kreisau and the Goerdeler groups had spent much time and energy sounding out people they thought fit to take the lead in each area after the Nazis' downfall.

Many Nazis considered it criminal so much as to think that Germany could lose the war, let alone discuss what would follow defeat. But, of course, while trying to ban such thoughts was impossible, Helmuth and his friends crossed the line between legality and illegality when they took such practical measures as drawing up lists of chief civilian representatives of a new provisional central government.

In August 1943 Helmuth drafted a document detailing 'Fundamental Principles for the New Order' and two sets of 'Instructions for the Land Commissioners'. The opening sentences of the 'Fundamental Principles', hammered out in discussion by the Kreisau group, were specific. 'The Government of the German Reich sees in Christianity the foundation for the moral and religious renewing of our people, for the surmounting of hate and lies, for the rebuilding of the European Community of peoples ... The main task now facing mankind in Europe is to get this divine order recognized. The solution lies in the resolute and vigorous realization of Christian values.'

The document went on to urge that freedoms of belief, worship and teaching be guaranteed. The Christian contribution was to receive a proper place in all cultural activities as well as film and radio. Most importantly, the relationship of the Reich with the German Evangelical (Protestant) Church and with the Roman Catholic Church would be regulated anew in friendly harmony. Here Helmuth made a concession because he wished to deny to the State any standing in the sphere of morality and to dissociate the German Churches from the State. In this way nobody would be able to excuse himself for committing an immoral act by saying it was enjoined, or not prohibited, by law. His argument was, 'The State is amoral because it is abstract.'

*

The verdict of the court in the case of Moltke was death and confiscation of property. When called on to make his final statement Helmuth told Freya he longed to quote Luther's hymn,

> And though they take our life,
> Goods, honour, children, wife,
> Yet is their profit small;
> These things shall vanish all,
> The city of God remaineth.

He refrained only because he feared that to parade such 'unquenchable truths' before 'these Romans' as he called them, would have been more damaging to the others.

Helmuth was proud that among all the prosecutions of members of the German Widerstand his own became the classic case for the supreme importance of the spirit. Freya said thirty-two years later, 'He was grateful – since he had to die – that he could die for being a Christian.'

Helmuth had written to her after the trial, 'This emphasis on the religious aspect of the case corresponds with the real inwardness of the matter and shows that Freisler is, after all, a good judge. He has unwittingly done us a great service in so far as it may prove possible to spread this story and make full use of it. And indeed in my view this should be done both at home and abroad. Our case-histories provide documentary proof that it is neither plots nor plans but the very spirit of man that is to be hunted down.'

Helmuth was appalled by the anonymity of death suffered by many of the Widerstand in Germany. In an analytical document which he wrote on a visit to Sweden in 1943 he declared, 'The worst is that this death is ignominious. Nobody really takes much notice of the fact, the relatives hush it up, not because there is anything to hide but because they would suffer the same fate at the hands of the Gestapo if they dared to tell people what had happened. In the other countries suppressed by Hitler's tyranny even the ordinary criminal has a chance of being classified as a martyr. With us, it is different: even the martyr is certain to be classed as an ordinary criminal. That makes death useless and therefore an effective deterrent.'

*

Between 1929 and 1945 Helmuth wrote 1,600 letters to Freya in his Lilliputian handwriting, and she preserved all of them. Although Kreisau was never searched, she found ingenious hiding-places. His letters were hidden in the bee-hives, and other documents were concealed in the rafters beneath the slate roof of the khaki-washed Schloss. There was no great risk of censorship. From Berlin his letters would have been difficult to identify, and at the village post office in Kreisau, no one dreamed of interfering with Frau von Moltke's letters. Even if they had been opened and any part of them deciphered, it is unlikely that these simple country folk would have understood much of what Helmuth was writing about. As an extra safeguard he used abbreviations, codewords and cover names to confuse those who might pry upon his neatly compressed handwriting.

Their daily letters to each other had to be confined to trivia during the eight months he was imprisoned at Ravensbrück, mainly a women's concentration camp with a new wing for political prisoners. When the security service were investigating the Kreisau circle after Stauffenberg's bomb attempt, Moltke was moved to Tegel, a civilian prison in the north-west suburbs of Berlin, where he found Pastor Harald Poelchau. He was one of the Widerstand who had escaped incrimination and had been appointed Protestant chaplain to the prison, the first such post to be created by Hitler. Not only was the pastor able to minister to his friends in their last hours but also to smuggle out their letters.

*

Freya Deichman, the daughter of a Rhineland banker, was an 18-year-old student when Helmuth first met her in August 1919 at a holiday home on the Grundlsee in Styria run by Dr Eugenia Schwarzwald. Founder of a progressive school, and one of the first women in Europe to become a doctor of philosophy, Dr Schwarzwald liked to gather round her the talented and the intelligentsia. She became convinced that Helmuth and Freya, who had grown up in a genuinely liberal tradition, would make a good marriage.

Freya was Helmuth's ideal complement, the Frau Doctor thought, contributing just those qualities which he lacked, such as optimism, gaiety and spontaneity. Freya's future mother-in-law was to echo those feelings, 'She's just right for Helmuth.' She effervesced with fun and enthusiasm. 'When Freya stops talking,' her future father-in-law once said, 'she stops living!' Not that there was anything superficial or weak about her character. Later, after their marriage, when strangers inadvertently called Helmuth 'Herr Doctor' it delighted him to point out their mistake: the doctorate belonged to his wife; she gained the degree of Doctor of Law from Berlin University in 1935. Helmuth never started to study for a doctorate. He always worked hard but looked upon knowledge principally as an aid to action.

Helmuth had an eminently practical mind and his mother's intending visit to South Africa in the first half of 1932 may have influenced the timing of the wedding. Freya could step in and manage the household in her absence! So Helmuth and Freya married on 18 October 1931, the wedding anniversary of Helmuth's parents and the golden wedding-day of his grandparents. And more like a daughter than a daughter-in-law Freya slipped easily into the political and social milieu at Kreisau.

Later Freya capably managed the household and the war-time 'house-parties' of the Kreisau circle. The food alone meant careful forward planning, as Helmuth was scrupulous about sticking to rations. 'If we're going to defy the Government over big things we must be sure to keep its rules over little ones.' Right to the end she kept Kreisau 'a haven of peace' for Helmuth, who had a deep love of the countryside, and for 'the little sons' as their father always called them. Helmuth described three days spent at Kreisau in June 1942 as 'precious green islands in a torrent'. Often his thoughts turned to the place, 'the shrubbery, the stones for the wall, the walnut trees, the cherry trees to be planted on the slope, the root crop harvest, food for the bees'. There was the danger that he might allow himself to escape from reality, but he realized this. 'Kreisau and everything about it, lovely and lovable as it is, is a distraction and I have got to get the better of this affair.'

Freya never tried to keep him at her side. Although separated for more time than they spent together, their sense of oneness was absolute and seemed almost impervious to partings. Helmuth was to write to Freya just before he died, 'You are my thirteenth chapter of the First Epistle to the Corinthians. Without you I would have "had not charity" ... You are that part of me which would be missing were I alone ... Only in union do we two constitute a human being .. We are one creative thought ... And so I am certain that you will not lose me on this earth, not for a moment.'

*

At the end Helmuth's faith shone like a diamond. His war-time experiences had undoubtedly combined to deepen his religious beliefs. His parents were Christian Scientists, but while bringing up their family in a religious atmosphere they did not impose their views. Helmuth had never practised Christian Science, nor did he appear at the time of his wedding a dedicated Christian. He and Freya planned a civil ceremony and it was only 'out of respect for the family' that they agreed at a late stage to a church service.

He was christened and confirmed as a Lutheran and when he took over the management of Kreisau he was responsible for maintaining both the Evangelical (Protestant) and Catholic churches on the estate. But he seldom went to church, and his mother's death in 1935 hit him hard because at that time he had no convictions about an after-life.

In March 1940 Helmuth had written to Freya, 'I read the Bible again for a bit, an activity in which I took more pleasure than ever before. Previously I regarded it as so many stories, at any rate the Old Testament, but today it is all real. It holds my attention differently from before.' In December 1941 he wrote with pleasure about a new friend in the Widerstand. 'Within ten minutes of starting to talk we got on to the subject of religion. This always happens with people who really shared my views.' (The friend was Carlo Schmid, a law teacher from Tübingen, who was working in the German Military Government at Lille. Schmid, who was half-French, began to act as intermediary between Helmuth's friends and the French Resistance. He was to play a distinguished and honourable part in post-war politics as a Social Democrat). It was an impressive fact that all the most determined members of the Widerstand were, or became, convinced Christians.

Helmuth was certain by 1943 that a Christian approach was the road for a new Germany to take. 'We must reawaken in the individual the awareness of owing a personal allegiance to values which are not of this world. Nothing else will make possible the restoration of his freedom. In this way the individual will recover an awareness of responsibility which will enable a feeling of true community to blossom.'

During his year's imprisonment (January 1944 to January 1945) Helmuth had twice become deeply depressed. Norman Poelchau, the chaplain, wrote to Helmuth's brother-in-law, 'He overcame it and during those months he penetrated to the very heart of Christianity. He fought his way through to the point where he was able to discern as God's handiwork what we ordinarily call ill-luck, political wickedness or human malice.'

Helmuth marvelled at the demonstration he had been given of God's presence and omnipotence. 'He shows them to us quite unmistakably precisely when he does what we don't like ... We must needs be overwhelmed when we suddenly realize that he has gone before us our whole lives through as a pillar of cloud by day and of fire by night, and that in a flash he suddenly lets us see it.'

During the thirteen days between the death sentence of the court and his execution on January 23, 1945, at Plotzensee, two and a half miles away from Tegel Prison, Helmuth took leave of his beloved Freya again and again in tenderly expressed letters, and at the same time he kept planning new applications to Himmler for a reprieve.

*

Freya worked hard to help them all. During both imprisonment and trial she got messages through to Helmuth and the other defendants. She went between Kreisau and Berlin and spent much of her time where she felt near to Helmuth, in the household of Pastor Poelchau, the valiant young chaplain from Tegel Prison. She beat on many doors; wrote to Himmler, notorious Chief of Police, who controlled both the SS and the Gestapo; and early in October 1944 she called upon Heinrich Müller, chief of the Gestapo, at the forbidding headquarters of the Security Service in Prinz Albrecht Strasse in Berlin.

Helmuth thought an interview with General Müller might help to save his life; but when Freya saw 'Gestapo Müller' he told her, 'We're not going to make the same mistake as in 1918 and leave our internal enemies alive.'

Her recollection of the visit is stark. 'Müller talked to me for about half-an-hour. He was polite, even friendly. I had to pretend I knew nothing of what the Nazis were accusing Helmuth. Müller told me I would be horrified to know what Helmuth had done.

'He left no doubt that he wanted Helmuth killed although he promised to talk to him personally. The trial before the Volksgericht would give Helmuth a chance to justify his actions. Müller felt that the Security Service had been treating Helmuth well – before the 20th of July 1944 when he was in Ravensbrück in prison for having warned a friend of his imminent arrest – and that Helmuth had been very disloyal.

'Müller was almost offended. He did not take Helmuth completely seriously, however, regarding him as a philosopher and no

man of action. He left me free to stay by Helmuth but said I could
not blame the Security Service for accusing him.'

Freya left Müller resenting the wedge he had tried to drive
between Helmuth and herself. This had made her say to Müller,
'Whatever he has done I will always bring up his sons to respect
and admire their father.'

Suddenly Müller came running after her in the corridor. 'After
it is all over, will you come back to see me? I'll then tell you
everything. We are not as bad as our name.'

General Müller saw Helmuth on 17 October 1944, but did not
change his mind about him.

*

Helmuth wanted his two final letters, or 'reports', to become an
object-lesson. 'I must remain the chief character, not because I am,
not because I want to be, but because otherwise the story loses its
thread. I have simply been the vessel for which God has taken
such endless trouble ... The task for which God created me
stands completed. This in no way alters the fact that I would
gladly go on living but then I should need a new commission.'

A letter to Freya dated 10 January considers a spiritual legacy.
'If you get the feeling of absolute security, should the Lord vouch-
safe it to you, which you would not have had without this time
and its outcome, then I am bequeathing you a treasure which no
man can take away, against which even my life cannot weigh in
the balance.'

On the eve of his execution he wrote to his family and friends
'Am I not fully entitled to read the 118th Psalm appointed for this
morning? 'O give thanks unto the Lord, for he is gracious: because
his mercy endureth for ever.'

Andrew Kaguru

1903–1953

Choice is the touchstone of true martyrdom and separates martyrs from victims. A martyr exercises his will, although he might affirm that God's will and his have become indivisible; but a victim is on the scene when violence erupts and becomes the casualty of circumstance. Sometimes it could be argued that the victims would not have been present unless they had been Christians, such as missionaries to the Third World. At the time of the Mau Mau uprising in Kenya many could have saved their lives either by denying their faith, or by taking one or other of the oaths. Other Christians were murdered simply to satisfy private revenge.

All the martyrs whose stories are recorded here had the opportunity to avoid violent death by running away, or recanting, or failing to bear witness; but knowing the likely penalty, decided to stand their ground. The classical and popular understanding that martyrs are good Christian men and women who died for their faith is acknowledged. Modern usage which enfeebles the word to encompass anyone who suffers from adhering to any belief or cause, or as a consequence of devotion to some objective, is discounted. In the discussion about bringing in the death penalty for terrorism the objection is invariably voiced that the dead terrorists would thus become martyrs. But it would be preposterous to class fanatics who toss bombs into crowded pubs and are then hanged for it alongside St. Stephen and St. Sebastian. It is the cause and not the death that makes a Christian martyr.

Andrew Kaguru, Kikuyu evangelist, was faced with an immediate and straightforward choice. He must either take the Mau Mau oath and retreat into the pagan society from which the Kikuyu had recently emerged, or die. The humble African never doubted that his martyrdom was the design of God. His faith was profoundly simple, and he told his wife, 'Nothing can happen to us unless God wills it.'

The Kikuyu boy half-ran, half-slid, the four miles to Kanyenyaini Police Station. The February night was dank with the mist which hangs over the Aberdare range and has a pungent smell like spent fireworks. Dawn would soon bring light to the strange shapes of familiar landmarks. The boy knew he dared not be seen by the Mau Mau watching from the forest where the trees seemed to clench black fists in anger. He tried to move secretly. Pastor Samuel Muhoro had whispered, 'If you're not too afraid, run, tell the police.'

Fear had kept him shivering in bed, naked and uncovered. The terrorists had taken his clothes and blankets, but after seeing what had happened to his mother he was determined to report the brutal attacks. Danson was twelve years old and the events of the night of February 14, 1953, were etched in his memory. His innocent young eyes had seen the drama like a camera, sharply but without comprehension.

The battering on the door at two in the morning had startled him from sleep in the family's mud house at Kiruri, an isolated village clinging to a shelf eight thousand feet up the mountains. Loud angry voices were shouting at his parents. They must swear the Mau Mau oath of hatred and vengeance, or die.

Danson had often heard his father, Andrew, denounce Mau Mau from the pulpit. Andrew's inseparable friend, Pastor Samuel Muhoro, who lived close by, also preached vehemently against the secret society. The boy thought it was the white man they wanted to drive out; but, he realized, it was also African Christians who were in danger. They, it was said, divided the tribe by adopting a 'foreign' religion in place of old tribal customs.

Danson knew Mau Mau initiation was by an oath taken secretly, by men, women and children, often administered by force and at night. This was contrary to Kikuyu law and tradition by which an oath must be taken in public, in daylight and voluntarily, and never by women or children.

The boy had trembled as he heard the terrorists beating his father. He knew his father would never swear. Nothing would make him, not even the thought of his wife nearing her time with their new baby and sixth child. When he married Wanjiku, the young Kikuyu girl whose parents were not believers, she was baptized Alice and became a Christian.

Alice had been conscious of the danger closing in and frequently implored her husband, 'Don't go far, don't be late tonight, take care.' The commonplace wifely words came with an urgent prayer, but Andrew always answered them with a calmness and a detachment which frightened his son. 'Nobody can take us from the hands of God unless he has God's permission. So let us go on until our work is finished.'

The beating did not go on for long before the leader called a halt. Then the men robbed the house. They entered the children's bedroom and collected their blankets and clothes. Danson's younger brother began to cry and he was hit on the head with a panga, the broad-bladed knife which everyone carried to use in the fields and to chop firewood. The wound drew blood. In the dark the raiders used torches and Danson could not identify any of them.

After looting the house, they returned to Andrew, who had been securely tied, and again the boy heard their leader urge his father to take the oath. His father insisted he could not because he was a true Christian. He was given five minutes to reconsider. Danson was terrified because he knew his father would not waver. 'I have no other decision,' his father said, his faith firm as a rock. The leader ordered the gang to take the evangelist outside and at the back of the house they beat him again. Danson heard his father groaning and soon everything was quiet, except for the laugh of hyenas.

Around four o'clock he heard his mother call him to light a fire. The Mau Mau had taken the lamp and he failed to get a fire going. He went into his mother's room. She lay on the floor, her limbs in pools of blood, and she bled too from a cruel gash in the neck. When he saw all she had suffered from the vicious beating, his fear left him. He summoned the courage to go outside and at the back of the house found his father's body. It had been hacked to pieces. He told his mother, and, although in great pain, she managed to crawl from the house to her husband's side to make sure there was nothing she could do. 'Danson, hurry. Tell the pastor,' she whispered.

The boy searched for something to wear and found a heap of clothes overlooked by the men. He ran to Samuel Muhoro's home and found the door broken down. With a child's deference for the pastor, he knocked all the same. The familiar voice called him to enter and he saw that the terrorists had also half-murdered Samuel.

In some places his body was slashed to the bone, and on his arm had been carved the initials M A U.

*

The terrorist organization, Mau Mau, had spread among the Kikuyu like fire in the bush, and caused the British Government to declare a State of Emergency in Kenya on October 20, 1952. At that time the Kikuyu numbered about half the country's Africans. They had a weakness for intrigue and many hoodlums whose only object was to make a living out of aggression were attracted to the obnoxious secret society; but there were other fundamental reasons for its hold on the tribe.

No one knows the meaning of the name, Mau Mau; it may have been a corruption of an African phrase, a Kikuyu version of 'aye aye', or just an ugly gobbling sound calculated to awaken fear. The society was no sudden explosion of violence but had its origins in the impact of civilization on a primitive people and the ruthless exploitation of subsequent tensions by its ringleaders. Grievances, both real and imaginary, resulted from the inevitable loosening of tribal ties caused by an imported religion and European culture. While some tribes accepted the white man's arrival more readily than others, the Kikuyu resisted firmly, and were most feared by the authorities, who suspected that when these tribespeople became educated they would replace their medicine men by political agitators.

For hundreds of years the Kikuyu had inhabited the densely forested area around Fort Hall, now Murang'a. They had no 'chief' system such as prevailed in other parts of Africa; their land was cut by deep watercourses and each ridge was controlled by a council of elders.

A burning grievance of the Kikuyu was land ownership, for this to the African was the basis of 'social security'. Grazing was vital for the gift of sheep, goats, and sometimes cattle, by the groom's family to the bride's and as a 'pension' in old age. Also, ancestral spirits were believed to dwell in the tribal lands and to continue to exert their influence there. The system of land tenure gave the Kikuyu rights to live on, or to cultivate, their family estates, and these rights were exercised through the heads of the family groups. Family estates, or *githaka*, could not be disposed of, although a Kikuyu could, with permission and upon payment of rent, farm in the *githaka* of another family.

Around the turn of the century four major disasters hit East Africa. Smallpox, rinderpest, drought, and locusts ravaged the population, their beasts and their crops. Many Kikuyu left the Kiambu district, the source of vast quantities of grain and beans, during the famine years. When they returned, some of the land they claimed as their own had been assumed by the Government to be abandoned and was occupied by European settlers. Instead of being landowners many Kikuyu were now employed as resident farm labourers, even though as well as wages they had their own areas of land for crops and grazing.

*

Andrew Kaguru's father once laboured on a farm in Solai and Andrew was the 'turkey-boy', looking after the birds for a few shillings a month. He was a quick intelligent lad who soon turned his hand to any job on the farm and more than earned his meagre wage.

When the owner of the land, a pioneer European settler, Frank Watkins, died, his son-in-law and daughter, Mr. and Mrs. J. K. Hill, moved to a large estate at Subukia in the Rift Valley, three days' journey by bullock wagon up-country, and they took Andrew with them. The Hills' daughter, Mollie, remembers Andrew from her childhood spent there. He became her father's head-man and was in charge of a hundred African labourers and 500 head of milking cattle. He also helped teach at the school which was started on the farm and had Church classes.

Shortly before she was twenty-one, Mollie became a Christian. Suddenly she realized what was meant by 'the African's lethal sense of humiliation'. 'We used to call the African labourers "nyama" which meant meat. Soon after my conversion Andrew brought a delegation of servants to see me. I didn't know their language – only 'kitchen Swahili' – but Andrew had a good smattering of English. He asked me why I had changed. They all noticed I was different. I told him I had become a Christian which explained my new attitudes and I apologized for the way I had treated them. Andrew stayed behind when the others left and we prayed together, the first African I prayed with. He was so loving and understanding.'

*

Another deeply felt grievance of the Kikuyu arose from a firm and foolish stand against one of their tribal customs made by the Church of Scotland Mission in 1929. The Mission ordered their schoolteachers to promise to abandon the practice of female circumcision.

The circumcision, or trimming the genital organs of both sexes, was to the Kikuyu an essential element of their culture, signifying the rite of passage from childhood to adulthood. Participation in the tribe's governing groups started from the day this operation, known as *irura*, was performed. It is fascinating to discover that tribal historical events and legends were recorded according to the names given to the different age-groups at the time of the initiation ceremony. If a famine occurred one year, for instance, that particular *irura* group would be known as 'famine' (ng' aragu). So if this custom were abandoned a tribe without written records would have no continuing diary of milestones in the life of its people. It was understandable that the Kikuyu suspected it was the secret objective of some missionaries – who were appalled at the surgical side of *irura* – to destroy their centuries-old social order and accelerate their Europeanization.

So much resentment of the dogmatic ruling of the Church of Scotland Mission was aroused that in October 1929 a school of the Gospel Mission at Kambui was pulled down by Kikuyu. Then, in a further eruption of violence soon afterwards, an elderly woman missionary, Hulda Stumpf, of the Gospel Mission, was mutilated and killed. Men broke into her home and performed on her the tribal operation of clitoridectomy as a prelude to her murder, which may have been unintentional.

This savagery was a sinister portent for the future.

*

Kenyatta, reputed leader of Mau Mau, known across Africa as 'Burning Spear', and the man who became Kenya's first President in 1964, was himself a product of the Church of Scotland's Mission to the Kikuyu Reserve. He first came to them as a boy of ten suffering from a spinal disease. An orphan from a forest *shamba* (smallholding) in the Fort Hall area, he gave his name as Kamau wa Ngengi. Two British missionaries operated on him and saved his life. He asked to be christened John Peter after the apostles but the missionaries told him that he could have only one name so he changed Peter to 'stone' and became Johnstone.

*

Now missionary disapproval of certain Kikuyu customs, particularly polygamy and female circumcision, led to indigenous break-away Christian sects. These reflected the strong nationalist and religious tendencies of the Kikuyu, and the new sects were vehicles for religious expression which adopted and yet adapted Christianity while retaining some tribal traditions. Ironically, the Scottish Mission had set in train events which were to be an important stimulus to Mau Mau.

The clamour for the opening of private schools run by Africans was led by the anti-European Kikuyu Central Association (KCA). Its general secretary was Kenyatta who in 1938 relinquished his baptismal name and took that of Jomo.

The outcome was the creation of two separate bodies, the Kikuyu Independent Schools Association (KISA) and the Kikuyu Karinga Education Association (KKEA). The first tried to keep a religious and non-political basis. The second was opposed to Government or Mission control and was completely secular. Through its schools and affiliated African Orthodox Church, a separatist organization outside the sphere of the European missionary societies, the KKEA provided the framework which enabled Mau Mau leaders to organize the spread of their terrorist movement.

The Kikuyu were quick to realize that education was the key to power and the political agitators soon saw that the independent schools could offer a superficially respectable front for subversion. The fact that the responsibility for their conduct lay with the Department of Education tended to camouflage the influence of Mau Mau. The Government was so short of inspectors that these schools had little if any supervision.

Although they became centres of disaffection, the effect on the Kikuyu tribe of the pupils of the KKEA schools was probably exaggerated. They were not good enough to foster leaders, nor numerous enough to be a strong influence. The KISA schools out-numbered them by five to one but agitators obtained control of these schools too late to do more than inculcate disloyalty among some of a single generation of juveniles. More important was their use of the school buildings and manipulation of the managing bodies as foci for the spread of Mau Mau. Nearly all school-teachers received threatening notices and some were murdered.

Meantime an ever-increasing population in the Reserves led to more and more pressure on the land, in large measure due to the agricultural methods and medicines of the whites which changed the old balance of nature. Kenyatta saw the exploitation of this 'land hunger' as the way to antagonize the Kikuyu against the Government and the European settlers. In fact, the area of land used for European settlement was a mere 110 square miles, and the Government, by accepting the recommendations of the Carter Commission into land grievances in 1933, made full restitution. However it was claimed by Kenyatta that no fewer than 110,000 Kikuyu had to live mostly as squatters on European farms outside the Reserves, and this fact was accepted in evidence to the Commission. Moreover the Kikuyu were aggrieved that the farms of the White Highlands broke the continuity of their lands. Also, under their system of land tenure their estates could not be got rid of because they were ancestral holdings. So no Kikuyu dispossessed of land by Europeans could believe this was more than a temporary arrangement.

Land was a cause of bitterness when Jomo Kenyatta returned to Kenya in 1946 after fifteen years spent in Europe. During this time he had studied anthropology at London University and was also an intermittent student at the London School of Economics. He had visited Moscow, learned Russian, and was a delegate at a number of Communist-sponsored African congresses in Europe.

The probable existence of a Kikuyu 'secret society', which aimed to annihilate Europeans, was reported by the District Commissioner for Fort Hall in December 1947.

*

The next year Andrew Kaguru, who had become farm manager for the Englishwoman, Mrs. Hill, after the death of her husband, left Subukia to become one of Christ's evangelists in Kikuyu country. (Mrs. Hill, herself attacked by the Mau Mau, later sold the farm and retired to South Africa). He returned to his birthplace of Kiruri in the Aberdare mountains, where as evangelist and lay reader he became the leading spirit of the small yet strong community.

Andrew loved the little grey stone church of Kiruri which the people had built for themselves from local materials. It was full every Sunday and often more people would stand outside to join in the rousing revivalist hymns and to listen intently to the preacher. This would either be the pastor, Samuel, or Andrew, who as lay reader was empowered to preach and to take services. Both men were vehement in their condemnation of Mau Mau.

Andrew delighted in the pastoral scene. A couple of hundred modest homes were built on the steep slopes, brilliantly coloured with tea bushes and golden wattle. Wild flowers pushed obstinately out of rocks where soil had eroded or from paths of hard red earth. There were clusters of 'bright eye', wild gladioli, gorgeous lilies, and, above the forest line, drifts of delphiniums. Boys herded cows, goats and brown hair sheep over the precipitous hillside. Tall blue gum trees reached hands to heaven and smoke seeped from the thatched roofs of the round huts warmed by open fires in the middle of the floor.

The Kikuyu Reserve was 'gospel country'. Christ could well be imagined here, as in the Holy Land, performing miracles, telling parables, resisting his temptations. In the Kikuyu setting the Bible stories came alive and the cost of discipleship was written in fiery letters at the time of the Mau Mau insurgence and its unholy demands. Andrew felt close to his personal heaven in Kiruri, and it seemed as if the whole world stretched out in front of him.

But he was aware that his home was dangerously near Mau Mau hide-outs all along the forest-line, and the terrorists must have suspected he had built his own network of 'intelligence' and knew their movements too well. He was notorious as an incorruptible Christian and, the Mau Mau knew, would not hesitate to go to the police. He would be judged a suitable case for murder because he was an activist and a natural leader. He was a dynamo of nervous energy which, harnessed to his practical resourcefulness, meant that he was a formidable adversary.

A few large mission stations became 'cities of refuge' where people in special danger lived together for mutual protection and fellowship. So those living in a cordon of Christian 'communes' up in the Kikuyu hills prepared their defences, both spiritual and practical, against the onslaught of the Mau Mau. The inhabitants of Kiruri were fifteen miles from the nearest mission 'refuge' but were also determined to ensure that their children had opportunities for education. They built the local primary and intermediate schools with their own labour.

The unordained and often untrained evangelists in charge of each local church were frequently teachers on week-days and church leaders on Sundays. They were singled out for attack by the Mau Mau and a number had already been murdered as part of a ruthless and effective plan to undermine the influence of the young Kikuyu Church at a crucial time.

Many took the Mau Mau oath as a form of insurance before they knew the extent of its evil.

*

The Mau Mau oath as a means to dominate the Kikuyu probably first came into existence soon after Jomo Kenyatta's return to the country. In the early days there was little abhorrent about the ceremonies; they adapted or perverted Kikuyu customs, and the oath was almost identical with the original one taken by members of the Kikuyu Central Association which pledged them not to give away the secrets of the society, not to sell land to strangers, not to help the Government arrest fellow-members. But there were also positive clauses obliging them to give money when called upon and to go to the help of members when asked to do so.

The Mau Mau leaders fully exploited the primeval fears underlying oath-taking to advance their evil campaign. In many Kikuyu religious ceremonies an arch of sugar cane and banana leaves was used, particularly in initiation rites at puberty. Mau Mau candidates had to pass through such an arch but the banana stems were used in other ways too. They were hollowed out to hold blood and a sheep's eye impaled at either end. Other paraphernalia of magic included sodom apples – tempting to look at but rotten at the core – threaded on twigs, calabashes holding blood and earth, and the root of a wild plant.

Soon dark tales of more sinister practices by the 'inner circle' of Mau Mau were circulating. There was even a strong rumour, never authenticated, that one of ex-Senior Chief Koinange's sons had been used as a human sacrifice.

Now with the onset of active terrorism two new versions of the oath were devised. The first called the *githaka*, or forest oath, was administered by forest gang leaders to their followers; the second, the *batuni* or platoon oath, was sworn by all Mau Mau soldiers. The worst of its vile excesses ordered the recruits 'to kill, no matter who is to be the victim, even one's father or brother'.

As the oaths became increasingly bloodthirsty, the rituals became utterly depraved. The use of menstrual blood and public intercourse with sheep and adolescent girls were common features and young women were kept with the gangs for this purpose. The foulest concoctions were eaten and drunk and it is not difficult to imagine the mesmeric effect of these orgies held in forest clearings by the flicker of bonfires. Later on in the emergency, when the forest gangs were on the run, cannibalism was introduced.

The tide of Mau Mau rebellion rose and by 1952 Government intelligence estimated that more than a quarter of a million Kikuyu had taken the oath and hundreds more were in prison for administering it or being present. These additions were made to the terms of the Mau Mau oath.

If I am sent with four others to kill the European enemies of this organization and I refuse, may this oath kill me.
When the reed-buck horn is blown, if I leave the European farm before killing the European owner, may this oath kill me.
If Jomo Kenyatta is arrested by our enemy I will die if I do not follow wherever he is taken and free him.
If I worship any leader but Jomo Kenyatta, may this oath kill me.

The authors of some publications inserted Kenyatta's name into hymns and prayers as part of the anti-Christian movement.

The African judiciary, with few exceptions, was patently corrupt and those who were not members of Mau Mau had no hope of receiving justice. The intensive drive to increase membership of Mau Mau was accompanied by violent intimidation and terror.

On 30 September Sir Evelyn Baring was sworn in as Governor of Kenya. On 9 October, the day that Chief Waruhiu, one of the three leading Africans in Kenya, was murdered, the Governor sent a telegram to the Secretary of State recommending the declaration of a State of Emergency and the early arrest of Jomo Kenyatta and his associates.

In Kiruri the people appeared united but the Mau Mau shrewdly guessed that their good citizenship was largely due to the leadership of Andrew Kaguru, and affection for their beloved pastor, Samuel Muhoro, whom many regarded as a saint on earth.

*

Meanwhile, letters were pouring into the headquarters of the Church Missionary Society in London from more than a hundred of their missionaries working in Kenya.

One said, 'It seems that a chapter in the history of the Kikuyu Church is closing but not in defeat: for that little flock that remains loyal to its Lord is demonstrating a quality of living which authenticates the gospel.' Despite the persecution there were still people coming forward for confirmation. 'It is no light matter,' wrote another missionary, 'to receive word that one's name is on the list of those to be killed; but this has been the experience of quite a number of African padres and Christians.' How many of us would continue going to church, asked the C.M.S., if we knew that the penalty for doing so might be death or a severe beating?

News of the impact of the Mau Mau uprising on the young Kikuyu Church was making sensational headlines in British newspapers. 'Is there anything we can do to help?' asked many Christians in England. As an earnest of their fellowship and concern Canon Cecil Bewes, then Africa Secretary of the C.M.S., flew from London on a goodwill visit. He had worked as a missionary for twenty years among the Kikuyu and was one of the translators of the Bible into their language. That last Christmas his heart had been more with the Kikuyu than at home.

He brought with him a personal letter from the Archbishop of Canterbury, Dr. Geoffrey Fisher, and a recorded message from Dr. Max Warren, General Secretary of the C.M.S. The Archbishop wrote, 'From England there goes out a constant stream of prayer that you may be upheld in all perils, kept true to the Christian faith in all temptations, and that you may find God's peace even in the middle of your suffering ... The Church in Kenya has been tested in the fire of affliction; and indeed some have been found faithless; but in every affliction the disciples of Christ shine out with the light of his strength.'

They were pertinent words indeed. Religion in Kenya had wrought dramatic evidence that the gospel was more than a comforting and beautiful story. The emergency saw a purge of the new Chrisitans. In Cecil Bewes's own challenging words it was, 'the sharpest sword ever laid to the heart and conscience of man'. The faith of many was in the crucible, and those who saw religion as a fashion rather than a faith, or merely as a means to education or employment, would now be uncloaked as nominal Christians.

Canon Bewes arrived in Nairobi on January 5, 1953. There had been no welcome from the crowds of Kikuyu in Pumwani, the African location in the town, despite his fluency in their own language. Usually this won him friends and smiles, for it was rare for a European to speak Kikuyu rather than Swahili which was the 'lingua franca'. But now they looked hard and resentful and shouted taunts. Driving up-country to the Kikuyu Reserve – his only 'brief' to shake the hands of fellow-Christians under persecution – he found Fort Hall looking like a fort. There were barbed wire stockades. Policemen lined one side of the road, soldiers the other. There was a general air of readiness for trouble, with lorries and armoured cars coming and going among the tents of the Army, because this was the centre of the Mau Mau's terrain.

On February 13 Cecil Bewes spent the evening with Andrew Kaguru. Pastor Muhoro and a local schoolteacher were also with him, and the four men discussed the emergency, the reactions of the African Church, and the dangers in their own area.

As in England, so in Africa, there was much nominal Christianity. By the early 1950s it had become the 'done thing' to go to Church and to have a Christian name, and when applying for a job it helped to have a letter from a missionary. If you belonged to the Church you had a seal of respectability: the Church was synonymous with education and prestige. The popular fallacy grew, 'I am a Christian because I wear European clothes.'

Then, as the Mau Mau rising escalated, to be a declared Christian was to live dangerously. The heat was on and nominal Christians melted away like snow in Mombasa. Pastors, like miniature bishops, each one looking after a number of churches scattered over a large area, found themselves largely unpaid. The Church in the Kenya Highlands had built a membership of 22,000 since their missionary work began at the turn of the century but now, in 1953, the number was down to 800. Schools were almost emptied and there were villages where nearly everybody had succumbed to terrorism. The faithful eight hundred Christians were torch-bearers and became renowned for their constancy.

That evening in the now dangerously isolated village of Kiruri in Kikuyu country, Canon Bewes heard how congregations had been decimated. Many people just disappeared; others stayed away from fear. The leaders of Mau Mau took the psychology of their fellow tribesmen into their reckoning when they framed the oaths. A Kikuyu who took a solemn oath believed that he would be risking supernatural punishments upon himself or his family if he broke that oath or if he perjured himself. Nor would he be likely to arrange for a 'cleansing ceremony' before making his report to the authorities, because to be effective such a 'cleansing' must be carried out in public before many witnesses.

It became essential to coerce people to take the oath once they had been approached, even if they were unwilling, otherwise they would constitute a threat to the movement. Mau Mau made it clear that anyone who tried to backslide would be victimized if not murdered. In one church a dead cat dangled from the lectern as a portent and a threat.

The crisis in the Kikuyu country coincided with a movement of spiritual revival from Ruanda which brought new power to the faithful. These revivalists called themselves 'brethren' because they felt part of one family, and as a greeting touched each other's shoulders. At their meeting when someone recounted a triumph over temptation, they sang a chorus of praise and gratitude beginning, 'Glory, glory, hallelujah, Glory, glory to the Lamb.' This hymn, which became their 'signature tune', was often sung at the gravesides of the martyrs. The Kikuyu Christians at this time told their 'brothers' and 'sisters', 'Do not pray that we may be kept safe, pray that we may be kept faithful.'

Samuel and Andrew had been united against Mau Mau, condemning its paganism and savagery; but they suspected that some among their congregation had taken the murderous oath and would report their denunciations. They told Cecil Bewes, 'We reckoned we had the promise of God's protection and so we

weren't worried.' Then one of their church members was murdered and they searched the Scriptures to see if they were right.
'We read in St. Luke's Gospel, "There shall not an hair of your
head perish." But just before it said, "And some of you shall they
cause to be put to death." We realized that the real protection
given us was eternal protection so if any of us are put to death we
have a praise meeting.' For pastor and lay reader and the convinced African Christians such a death must have come by the
permissive will of God, because for them, nothing happens that he
does not allow.

Canon Bewes was deeply moved by Samuel and Andrew, 'ordinary men with extraordinary courage', whose implicit belief, uncomplicated by intellectual argument or deep theology, inspired
others among the common people. The sincerity of these two solid
African Christians was humbling.

The scene in the lonely village, high above the Maragua River
where the rainbow trout leaped, was tranquil, but Cecil Bewes
had seen enough of the country since his return to convince him
that it was an illusory peace.

He returned to Weithaga, fifteen miles down the mud road
from Kiruri. This was his old home and he always thought that it
must be one of the loveliest mission stations in the world, built
high on a hill on the lower slopes of the Aberdares. Here in 1900
'Bwana' McGregor had founded the first Mission in Kikuyuland.
(He had also started a school at Kiruri which Andrew had attended). Now Weithaga was the centre of a network of nearly a
hundred mission churches and schools and it dominated many
miles of the Reserve.

Canon Bewes slept in a small hut on the outskirts and admits he
was scared. The Mau Mau had burnt down huts only half a mile
away, giving the occupants the choice of staying inside to be
burnt alive or coming out to be hacked to death. Only later did he
discover that the faithful Kikuyu mounted vigil each night to
guard his hut.

The next day he was driving across country to Embu, where the
wild buffalo grazed, when police stopped him. They asked where
he had come from and then gave him details of brutal attacks in
Kiruri by the Mau Mau.

*

When Cecil Bewes was told by the police about the Mau Mau raid at Kiruri, he returned there at once but found nothing that he could do. The Weithaga Mission had soon heard by 'bush telegraph' and had fetched a nurse from Kanyenyaini. Andrew's body already lay in the mortuary at Fort Hall, about twenty-eight miles away where Andrew's eldest son, Danson, and his brother were taken to police headquarters to give information and to identify the body. Alice and Samuel and Sara Muhoro were in hospital there, but so badly injured that Cecil Bewes was not allowed to see them.

The next day the Revd. Neville Langford Smith, a schools supervisor and later bishop, and the Revd. Obadiah Kariuki, the rural dean (who was to become the first Kikuyu to be consecrated bishop in the Anglican Church) went with Danson and his uncle to collect Andrew's body. Then they joined others who were waiting in lorries at outlying places such as Kahuhia and Weithaga, to escort the body to Kiruri for burial.

Three hundred believers gathered at the church Andrew loved, its walls cut blocks of the grey local stone, and the beautiful wooden pews made painstakingly by village carpenters.

A worshipper described the scene. 'There was great praising when we met. The service was in church and then we marched to the grave singing "Onward Christian Soldiers" for the burial, and afterwards, "Loving Shepherd of Thy Sheep". Andrew was a saint; his life just reflected Christ.'

At Kiruri, with Kaguru dead and Muhoro in hospital, the congregation dropped off, but the church was kept going by a brave nucleus of five old ladies, led by Samuel's redoubtable mother. These five faithfully and regularly held prayer-meetings.

*

When the Archbishop of Canterbury, Dr. Geoffrey Fisher, visited Kenya after the emergency, he met Samuel Muhoro and said, 'I don't know what I should have done if I had been called upon to suffer torture as you were.' The pastor replied simply, 'Only God gave me the strength. I thank God for the power to endure which he gave us, because it must have been given just for that time, to enable us to speak in friendship to those who came to attack us.'

Describing the incident, he said he had been more fiercely attacked after each refusal to take the oath – by the time he and Andrew were ordered to take the Mau Mau oath, it had degenerated from a relatively innocuous form of political allegiance, to a 'killing oath' often administered with indescribably obscene and bestial embellishments – and finally, a sword was thrust into his back so that he thought they had cut his kidneys.

His wife, Sara, was ordered to quieten the crying baby, the youngest of their children who had all been made to look on. If the child did not stop crying, they said, she would be killed too. Later, they cut Sara about the head and snapped the little finger of her left hand. The house was stripped of everything except a single blanket to cover the infant and a surplice thrown over Samuel.

Samuel told the Archbishop how in the end it was the terrorists who trembled. For Samuel and Sara it was a miracle. They confessed that when they were being grievously wounded they felt neither pain nor despair. The pastor said he hesitated to talk about their ordeal in case people should think how wonderful they were. 'Then I remembered how I have been helped myself by the witness of others, like St. Stephen,' he said. 'We saw Jesus standing on our side. Our bodies were badly beaten and blood was flowing as water, but he was with us. He gave us words of love to speak to our persecutors, who said they didn't know we were "that type of God people" and asked for our prayers.'

*

When Mollie Hill (who became Mollie MacKenzie upon marriage) heard of Andrew's martyrdom her reaction was intensely practical. She sent money to support the baby safely delivered of Alice a few months after Andrew's death. He is named Samuel after Pastor Samuel Muhoro. Mollie, who left home to serve as a missionary in Ethiopia, wrote forty-six years later, 'Even now I would say that to have known Andrew Kaguru was one of the greatest influences and encouragements in all my Christian life. He became a fine evangelist.'

*

The author of the official Colonial Office Report (*Historical Survey of the Origins and Growth of Mau Mau*, May 1960), Mr. F. D.

Corfield, observes: 'It was most noticeable that the followers of Mau Mau were not drawn from those who were truly Christian nor yet from those who had remained true to the old Kikuyu religion. These two small minorities, both loyal to their respective faiths, had an immense influence and were the chief factors in the final defeat of Mau Mau in the Reserves ... The remarkable and heartening fact is that the true and fundamental tenets of Christianity have survived and surmounted these difficulties, and it is a tribute to many individual missionaries that so many Kikuyu have absorbed the fundamental teaching of Christ.'

Today at Kiruri, a fine 'Harambee' (meaning community achievement) secondary school stands on land opposite the little stone church which Andrew Kaguru loved. Pastor Muhoro is still there and has his time fully occupied with baptisms and confirmations, weddings and funerals as he ministers throughout the large area made a new parish in August 1975.

Alice Kaguru remains an ardent Christian and lives in a mud house thatched with leaves in four acres of land where many of her large family live. She still suffers physically from her beating by the Mau Mau. All her children are Christians and attend at church. The consecration of new churches is a regular feature on the Archbishop's calendar. The latest *Kenya Church Handbook*, which unfortunately has not been reprinted since 1973, reports that 73 per cent of Kikuyu are now Christians. Jomo Kenyatta, who died on August 22, 1978, and came to win respect in the West for his statesmanship, professed to be a Christian and was made a vice-president of the Bible Society. Here in Kenya the power and glory of the martyr are triumphant.

Vivian Redlich

1905–1942

May Hayman

1905–1942

Discretion knows no part of the valour of martyrdom. Fidelity is its hallmark and the real constancy lies in obedience to the will of God.

The English priest, Vivian Redlich, and his fiancée, Australian nurse, May Hayman, refused to leave when the dangers of war came to New Guinea because they were convinced their profession laid a special trust upon them to stay with their people, there and then. They had already determined to remain before their Bishop, Philip Strong, reminded his mission staff that God had prior claim on their obedience.

The Bishop's words went straight to the heart of the dilemma. 'No one requires us to leave. But even if they do, we should then have to obey God rather than man.' The Bishop reassured his workers, 'If we are all to perish in remaining, the Church will not perish, for there will have been no breach of trust in its walls. Its foundation and structures will have been strengthened by our faithfulness unto death.'

Yet no Christian can properly court martyrdom. Some are called by God, and their congregations, to run away, to enable them to discharge other commissions, for all have not the gift of martyrdom. True Christians are pliant and obedient to God's purposes for them and the conviction of the martyr springs from a call irresistible in its clarity for him.

Canon Basil Redlich had a financial struggle to support Vivian at Chichester Theological College, but it pleased him that his eldest son was to follow him into the ministry. The divide in their churchmanship – Basil Redlich was a modernist and Vivian adopted the Catholic tradition – did nothing to impair their relationship. His father had a ministry both in this country and in

South Africa. Vivian was born in Natal and he spent some time in South Africa on account of ill-health. From a child he was delicate and he would probably have failed today's medical for a missionary. Temperamentally he was nervous and highly-strung.

His childhood was spent happily in the Leicestershire countryside with his brother Nigel and sister Monica. His father, who was rector at Little Bowden, near Market Harborough, also wrote books of biblical scholarship and was at one time the director of religious education in the Diocese of Peterborough. Vivian's schooling was shared between England and South Africa and interrupted by bouts of ill-health. He grew into a lank pale man with a vaguely bird-like appearance lent by large round spectacles.

In 1926, shortly after his 21st birthday, he entered Chichester Theological College. Vivian had felt a calling to the mission field for some time and even offered to go to Tristan da Cunha. The Archbishop of Capetown advised him to seek ordination in England, and Canon Lionel Pass, the then Principal of Chichester, who was to become like a father to Vivian, was impressed by his 'clear idea of his vocation'. This appeared a lot stronger than his academic ability. His letters to his Principal written during vacations and sickness made frequent references to 'the dreaded terminals'. 'I look forward to being back except for the prospect of terminals ... I hope you've recovered from the shock which my terminal papers must have occasioned!'

His tutor, the Revd. Dr. Thomas Parker (afterwards Fellow of University College, Oxford), summed him up as essentially an active character without much intellectual curiosity. 'He was not lazy in his work, but the reading he regarded merely as a means to an admittedly good end – that of ministerial service.'

Vivian, it seemed, thought theology, except in its most elementary forms, rather a waste of time, and he certainly imagined there was a simple answer to every theological question. His father's books, which were designed to make theological ideas, especially new ones, available to the ordinary man, may have influenced this undue simplicity of outlook in his son.

Both Vivian and his tutor shared a passion for railways, a common clerical pastime, and out of a mutual enthusiasm for the hobby sprang a deep friendship.

'He was most pressing that I should go to New Guinea with him. I felt quite sure that my vocation lay in the academic field; but I rather think that Vivian thought it was running away from the call of God. This illustrates his singlemindedness. He was always sure what he was called to do, and I have no doubt, indeed, that he was destined by God for martyrom. But he was also rather apt to assume that he knew what God intended for others!

'I would have preferred him to have had an university education; but his slender academic background certainly did not hamper him becoming a fine priest. I suppose none of us foresaw the heroic end which was to be his, although I think that anyone who knew him would have expected him to meet any crisis with bravery and resolution, and indeed would have been surprised if he had not.'

There was, however, a lightheartedness about Vivian Redlich which was more apparent in those days than his saintliness. Fellow-students remember him best for his practical jokes. One recalled, 'It was rather difficult to take him seriously at times.' Not surprisingly, for he fitted a bell to his door which when pushed spouted a jet of water. He stuck a shilling piece to the floor of his room, and made a clockwork matchbox which scuttled away from anyone who tried to pick it up.

He was a skilled mechanic with cars and radios, and the house-man reported that Mr. Redlich's door was opened and shut by remote control. He made himself a 'cat's whisker' wireless set inside a match-box and built his own alarm-clock combined with a tea-maker. His spare time – and more – was spent on inventions.

Vivian's mother died in 1929 and in letters to his Principal Vivian revealed a deep faith in resurrection. He was much moved by his mother's death, and his doctor advised a break from studies. Vivian sailed to Canada to spend two years as a lay worker in the Rocky Mountains with a roving commission which appealed to his spirit of adventure. He visited remote farms in Northern Canada, bouncing along on rutted roads or rough grass on an Indian motor-cycle, a 499 c.c. Harley Davidson single cylinder which weighed over 3 cwt. 'A most admirable mount, but quite a load to pick up out of a snowdrift,' Vivian wrote to his College.

He returned to Chichester in May 1931 and the next year was ordained by the Bishop of Wakefield, Dr. James Seaton. At this time his college reported to the Bishop, 'He was rather young in his ways when he came to us, but since his return from Canada he has been quite a different person and has gained a really serious outlook on life. . . . He has a vocation and is really in earnest . . . he has been a real example to other men in spiritual things . . . he is a thinker but one of those people who probably can never do themselves justice in examinations.'

In fact he passed Part I of the General Ordination Examination but failed Part II. His Principal pleaded to the Bishop, 'he has not done *very* badly', and James Seaton agreed to ordain him if he passed the deacon's examination which he did.

Vivian's first charge was as curate at St. John's, Dewsbury Moor, in Yorkshire. It is one of the 'million churches' built under a Parliamentary grant in 1818 of a million pounds for churches in populous districts.

He brought great zest to his first curacy and quickly showed a flair for getting on with the youngsters of the parish. When pay day came he gave the children a party out of his own pocket, and was soon running a Scout troop. He found he was not 'much of a hand' at bible class and Sunday school was 'a bit of a bear garden', but the children loved him for all his nonsense. He certainly disabused them of any idea that to be 'religious' was to be dull.

Despite the College observations about his new serious outlook, Vivian still loved practical jokes. His visitor's overcoat fell to the floor because the hanger he offered was made of rubber, and anyone given a glass of water would take a shower because the glass had holes hidden in the pattern. When the Mothers' Union met, clockwork mice ran out from under their chairs. 'Flies' stuck on with pins decorated the cake for his Assistant Scoutmaster's wedding.

A strong Churchman as well as a Christian, Vivian demanded reverence in the service. He began one sermon by placing on the top of the pulpit all the sweet papers and other articles he had found in church after the last church parade.

The Bishop of Wakefield heard of his work with young people, and once, when returning from the Church Assembly in London, he ordered an astonished chauffeur to drive to 'the Den of the Dewsbury Moor Rovers'.

*

After two years Vivian felt impelled to enter the mission field, always his hope. 'Where do you want to go?' asked the Secretary of the Society for the Propagation of the Gospel in London. He did not know. While he was thinking, another clergyman walked into the office. 'I need a man for the Bush Brotherhood in Australia,' he said. The secretary introduced the young curate, and Vivian agreed to undertake a motor ministry thoughout the lonely lands of the semi-tropical diocese of Rockhampton on the coast of Queensland. He signed on to serve for five years and to stay single. His salary was to be £30 a year and keep.

Vivian Redlich sailed to Rockhampton in June 1935 and after a train journey of 400 miles reached Longreach where the Bush Brotherhood had started 40 years before. At first he went to help in the Dawson Valley. He wrote to his old parish, 'Our headquarters is Wowan where we go once or twice a month to collect mail. It is 50 miles from Rockhampton, consists of two hotels, three churches, a few shops and a butter factory. We camp in the vestry which is as comfortable as a hen coop ... Give us a thought sometimes in your prayers – we've got a pretty wearing job on. I don't forget Dewsbury Moor. I daren't think too much about it.' He had told the SPG Secretary before he left, 'All my Scouts want to come too! Can't you charter a plane and take us all?' In October he wrote to 'his boys', thanking them for gifts (he had sent them a boomerang for the 'Den'). 'Fifteen miles between homesteads is close, three miles positively overcrowding – in the far-out parts 60–90 miles is quite normal for neighbours ... My area is 100,000 square miles!'

Vivian made a portable altar for his travels, so that he could convert a veranda or front parlour into a chapel. He coaxed an old motor car over any road – or none! – and frequently chauffeured the Bishop of Rockhampton on long confirmation tours.

In 1940 his five years were up and he was due to come home; but Vivian Redlich heard another call. Dr. William Wand, then Archbishop of Brisbane and later to become Bishop of London, had consecrated a new Cathedral in Dogura the previous year and

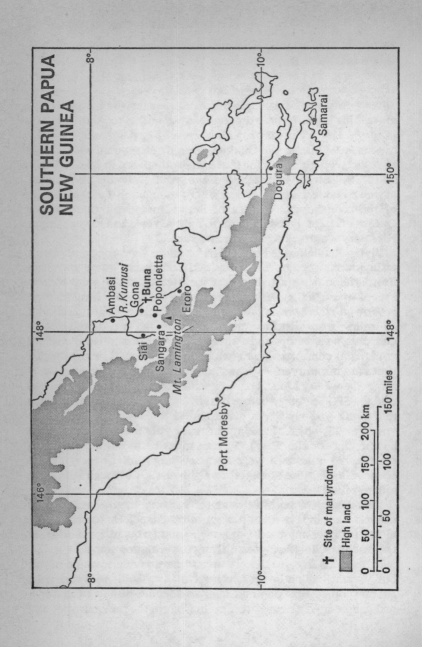

SOUTHERN PAPUA
NEW GUINEA

Ambasi
R. Kumusi
Gona
✝ Buna
Popondetta
Siai
Sangara
Eroro
Mt. Lamington
Port Moresby
Dogura
Samarai

✝ Site of martyrdom

High land

8°
148°
146°
10°
150°

0   50   100   150 miles
0   50 100 150 200 km

reported a shortage of priests and Christian workers in New Guinea. Vivian volunteered.

His first sight of the new country was Samarai, the 'Pearl of the Pacific', at the south-eastern tip where diocesan headquarters was housed and Anglican church supplies kept. This beautiful islet, which has a deep water wharf, was also Papua's commercial centre, with warehouses for unloading ocean-going vessels bringing supplies from Australia, China and Britain. Here in the small wooden church of St. Paul's he assisted the rector. He wrote home to his former vicar in Dewsbury Moor about his 'new boys', the brown Papuans who helped him to sort and count stores, 'One of my work lads has been sitting on my floor as I write, studying the pictures in the *Weekly Times*.' After a few days in this paradise island Vivian was sent off in the mission schooner to the east coast village of Taupota where he settled down to work and began to learn the language.

*

A year later, in 1941, the Anglican Mission to New Guinea celebrated its Golden Jubilee with a Service of Thanksgiving in Dogura Cathedral. On August 10, 1891, Albert Maclaren and Copland King, Anglican missionaries, had landed on the wharf at Wedau, Dogura. Warriors greeted them with spears poised, but their Chief was friendly, and bartered them land in exchange for tobacco and tomahawks. Tribes of cannibals used to fight on the Dogura plateau but here the two pioneers built a small chapel and their house. In the same spot, perched between a coral reef and wild mountains, the gleaming white cathedral of St. Peter and St. Paul was raised in the five years 1934–1939 by native labourers who worked without wages, and gave £500 towards the £4,000 which it cost.

Two days after the Jubilee celebrations, when Vivian Redlich was preparing to return to his village of Taupota, he was told by the Bishop that he was to be priest-in-charge of Sangara, the Inland Mission, a hundred miles north-west of Dogura. Vivian was overjoyed by the opportunity and a fortnight later he was there.

He wrote in characteristic staccato style to his father, then rector of Little Bowden, a village in the English Midlands. 'There

are two fine ladies here, Sister Margery Brenchley (nurse), Miss
Lilla Lashmar (teacher), but up till now no resident priest. It's a
pretty and busy place – school over 300 – big local population –
140 Christians and many catachumens nearly ready for baptism.
Coffee-growing – a big Government and native Co-op. affair.
Rubber nearby. We can even get from the beach thirty miles
away, to within twenty minutes of the Mission by motor truck . . .
I had a "Church Council" meeting last night, so my room still has
aroma of coconut oil (skin polish) and trade tobacco.'

Vivian's days were fully occupied with baptisms down at the
river, and schools to care for. He was also doing a lot of building,
'a swanky new hospital, teacher's house, stores, my house and
workshop.' He made a font of beaten brass for Sangara Church. It
was a rewarding outdoor life with plenty of outlets for his practical bent.

The war had not yet menaced the Far East but the new priest
was soon troubled by the scourge of sorcery in his parish. Its
influence was insidious and deep-seated and it seemed to Vivian
the devil's own work.

Not far from Sangara lived the sorcerer, Embogi. The mere men-
tion of his name terrorized the Papuans. He ruled tyrannically over
the Jegarata, a tribe of wild natives in the mountains, and his spies
were everywhere. Embogi tried to manipulate the murder of all
Christians because he was jealous of authority. Only he must rule
and he feared competition, particularly from the supernatural.
The Government suspected that Embogi and his gang were behind
every crime they had to punish. Once they imprisoned him at Port
Moresby, but Embogi escaped to resume with even greater vil-
lainy his roles of sorcerer and robber chief.

The Papuans were still living in the Stone Age and for thousands
of years had believed in their own spells and rituals, their own
ghosts. Native superstitions attributed all events, both cata-
strophic and beneficial, to the work of wizards and witches. Few
Papuans believed that anyone died a natural death, and most lived
in dread lest a sorcerer touch them stealthily by hand, or with
stick or stone, and so bring death. The feeling engendered by this
widespread belief in occult powers was one of terror. The missionaries offered another kind of magic, perhaps a Holier Ghost. On a
more mundane level Father Vivian, in battered straw sunhat and

pulling at an ancient pipe, was a very present source of practical help.

*

On 7 December 1941 the Japanese made a surprise attack on Pearl Harbor, the U.S. naval base in the Hawaiian Islands. America declared war; but the raid had destroyed most of the U.S. Pacific Fleet and the Japanese armies were soon sweeping through south east Asia, apparently invincible. By the end of the month they threatened New Guinea. The Japanese strategy was to transform the Western Pacific into a Japanese lake and to establish a line of defence which would include the Bismarck Archipelago off the north-east coast of New Guinea.

Early in 1942 Japanese warships were seen off the Papuan coast. On January 20 Vivian Redlich wrote to his father, 'Events have flared up; all women, barring missionaries and nurses, have been evacuated. We are agreed that we will stay put whatever happens.'

On January 23 the capture of Rabaul, on New Britain, the largest and most important of the islands forming the Bismarck Archipelago, brought danger nearer. The small but important port of Samarai, which was the supply point for the whole of south-east Papua, became an obvious target for attack. Its population was evacuated by Government order, and the diocesan headquarters transferred to Dogura, the Cathedral centre on the north-east coast.

Soon after the first air-raid on Samarai, a scorched earth policy was implemented. All the buildings were burnt down except St. Paul's. Three times the Army set fire to the church but although made of wood, it did not burn. A small scorch mark on a wooden pillar was the only damage and today this is encased in glass, a symbol of the indestructibility of the Church under fire.

Between the advancing Japanese Army and Port Moresby, the south coast capital and 'gateway to Australia', stood only the razor back of the Owen Stanley mountains, less than sixty miles across. An order went out, 'Hold at all cost, to permit preparation of mainland defences.' If Port Moresby fell, Queensland would come within range of Japanese bombers.

It was evident that most Anglican missionaries would soon be in the battle area. On January 31, the fourth Bishop of the Diocese, Philip Strong (afterwards Archbishop of Brisbane), broadcast to all staff of mission stations from Dogura which had the main transmitter. Those not equipped with radio received his speech by runners. 'Whatever others may do, we cannot leave. We shall stand by our vocation ... If we are fools, we are fools for Christ's sake.'

Bishop Strong lived up to his name in steely resolve. What he called his 'heart-to-heart' talk was devastating in its challenge. 'I have from the first felt we must endeavour to carry on our work in all circumstances, no matter what the cost may ultimately be to any of us individually. God expects this of us. The Church at home, which sent us out, will surely expect it of us. The Universal Church expects it. The tradition and history of missions requires it of us. The people whom we serve expect it of us. Our own consciences expect it of us. We could never hold up our faces again, if, for our own safety, we all forsook him ... Our life would be burdened with shame and we could not come back here and face our people again; and we would be conscious always of rejected opportunities.'

'The history of the Church tells us that missionaries do not think of themselves in the hour of danger and crisis ... His watchword is none the less true today as it was when he gave it to the first disciples – "Whosoever will save his life shall lose it, and whosoever will lose his life for my sake and the gospel's shall find it." '

Five years later, Bishop Strong was to tell his Diocesan Conference he believed the message had been divinely given him; but it was not the broadcast which decided the staff to stay at their posts. Letters from them to the Bishop suggested that God had inspired him 'to say what was already in the hearts of all'.

The Bishop himself was often under fire. Six weeks after his memorable broadcast the mission boat was bombed, and later Philip Strong was shot at by machine-guns while visiting territory in Japanese hands.

In the autumn the authorities demanded the evacuation of women missionaries and now the Bishop did not feel that the order should be resisted. By this time the whole of north-east Papua had become operational and was about to be used as a base for an offensive against the Japanese. 'I feel that our women missionaries have already made a witness that has been necessary and will not be forgotten and that their going at this stage will not have the same adverse effect on native morale and on the Papuan Church as if they had gone nine months earlier.'

The Bishop was also told that the authorities might order all his staff to go. He made it clear that men missionaries would leave only under force and the demand was not made.

In his Lenten Pastoral Letter of 1942 Bishop Strong declared, 'I have no doubt that the course we have adopted is the right one. I have never felt so certain about anything in my life. At each season of Lent, metaphorically we are called to go up to Jerusalem, but for us never more so than in this year ... We have entered what may well be the Lent of the Papuan Church.'

*

In Dogura Vivian Redlich waited impatiently to return to Sangara. He had had to return to headquarters for medical attention in June 1942. When he left in the mission schooner a month later, loaded with enough stores for six months, the Bishop warned him that he might encounter the Japanese. 'Well, that would be just too bad, wouldn't it?' the priest replied, trying hard to sound laconic.

In fact, the Bishop's words were prophetic. Redlich nearly ran into the Japanese invading army while they were shelling the beach at Buna on the north-east coast. He heard the brutal barrage of guns while he worked in the darkness to land fifteen tons of supplies and to hide them in the bush. He was out of sight around the headland from the Japanese. Wistfully he watched the M.V. *Maclaren King*, named after the first Anglican missionaries, sail out of Oro Bay to return to headquarters. It would have been easy to have gone back in the boat. His exuberant nature rebelled against the sacrifice which he knew might await him but he believed implicitly that he was there in the bush on God's work. To him, commission and commitment meant the same; his duty lay with his flock, both in good times and in bad.

'For better, for worse' ... perhaps the solemn words from the marriage service ran in his head as the schooner disappeared from view. Vivian had no wish to court martyrdom. At 37 he had much to live for and had just become engaged to May Hayman, a vivacious Australian nurse with long brown curls. She was stationed at Gona Mission, on the north-east coast, overlooking the Solomon Sea and fringing the jungle. They looked forward to an early marriage and starting a family.

May, whose father was a railway engineer, was the sixth child in a family of eight. She had been unhappy as a typist and so went to Adelaide to train as a nurse. When qualified she nursed at a large hospital in Canberra before going to Sydney to prepare to become a missionary. She had joined the New Guinea staff six years before.

May wrote home to Australia about her engagement. At first she had demurred. Their marriage might hinder the work they were both pledged to do. But Vivian was adamant, reassuring. 'I am convinced that my affection for you is not something apart from my work and yours but that the whole is inextricably bound up and that the whole future of my work and ministry is meant to be linked with you.'

On reading May's letter, her sister-in-law, Mrs. E. R. Hayman, remembered how the young nurse had nearly become engaged to a boy she had met in Canberra, but May had broken off their friendship because 'he had no religion and tried in every way to destroy her beliefs.'

Of her coming wedding to Vivian, she wrote in excitement, 'What more could any wife wish for! What a marvellous partnership! Vivian admits that although his priestly vocation is so sure, he has been troubled about his calling to this branch of the work. Now these doubts have quite vanished and he feels free to throw himself into a work that really does attract him.'

They were the same age, their ideas were very much alike, and she endorsed Vivian's dream of their 'future home, when and where . . .' He had written to her, 'Ours must be a friendly Mission. Everyone must be welcome and encouraged to use the place and yet not be over-pampered but made to learn to help the work. On one or two Mission stations some of the staff are rather inclined to push the natives off when church services and school are over. (Our own private bit must be limited but what there is of it must be very definitely our own). For long I've felt that while many missionaries are giving their services for their people, they don't live enough for them but too much for themselves. I know I have done. You'll have to cure me of this – and if necessary drive me out to my people.'

It was in the apricot light of the dawn that the *Maclaren King* sailed out of Oro Bay, and after the boat's departure Vivian made his way back to Sangara, some thirty-five miles inland, as quickly as possible. To avoid Japanese patrols, he went into hiding in the steaming jungle where the Papuans built him a lean-to shelter of leaves on the side of a hill near the village of Hondituru. They posted watchers along the track and brought food and news.

The Japanese had boasted to a village policeman, 'Tomorrow is Sunday. We will smash up the Mission.' The Papuan Christians crowded around their priest and asked, 'What shall we do?'

Vivian Redlich spoke quietly. 'I am your Father. I am not going to run away from you,' he reassured them. 'I shall say Mass tomorrow and anyone who wishes may communicate.'

At dusk he was joined in his bush shelter by an Australian friend. Harry Bitmead, a travelling medical assistant for the Papuan Civil Government, had been stationed in the Buna area for the past year and was in charge of a Government Medical Training School for Papuans at Isuga-Lambo, about forty minutes' walk from the Mission. Earlier that day Bitmead had escaped from the Japanese helped by one of the Sangara Mission boys. A native policeman had told him where Redlich was hiding. He thought the policeman lied because a month before the Japanese invaded, he knew that the priest had been taken sick and had had to be carried the distance to Dogura. Bitmead did not think it at all likely he would see him back at his post. The policeman insisted, 'Father came back to Oro Bay on the *Maclaren King* and walked into the Mission.'

Bitmead found the priest in his hide-out. 'He was a godsend to me. He gave me food and drink and told me to rest, while under cover of darkness he stole into the Mission to salvage altar vessels for Communion.'

By dawn a crowd of natives had gathered and waited to receive the Sacrament. The priest woke his friend and began to vest.

Suddenly, Andrew, a Papuan boy who was going to serve that morning, rushed in. 'Father, go quickly. Do not wait. During the night Embogi came to look for you. Now he's gone for the Japanese to come and kill you and Mr. Bitmead.'

Vivian Redlich bowed his head to pray. Then he said calmly, 'Today is Sunday. It is God's Day. I shall say Mass. We shall worship God. Why *has* Embogi done this? Does he hate us? Have we ever harmed him?' From here and there among the crowd came the murmur, 'Embogi is not a Christian.'

Redlich turned to Bitmead, a Roman Catholic, 'Will you remain for Mass?' 'Yes,' he said. 'But no sermon! Just the service.'

The English priest spoke in a low voice. 'Hear what comfortable words our Saviour Christ saith unto all that truly turn to him.' . . . Later Harry Bitmead described that last Mass. 'I do not think I have ever witnessed a more devout congregation. The fervour on those faces would have equalled that of the early Christians assisting at Mass in some hidden catacomb. Like them, these New Guinea Christians were assisting at Mass at the risk of their lives. The dense silence of the jungle was broken only by the sound of the priest's voice praying for his people.

'Then came the rustle of movement as those bare brown feet moved near the altar at the time of Communion. He who was about to go down to his own bitter Gethsemane and Passion, offered up for the last time before the throne of God for his people the saving sacrifice of Christ.

'As the sacrifice of Christ had its justification on Easter morning, so too, in God's own time, will the sacrifice of the loyal and devoted priest, Vivian Redlich.'

The service over, Harry Bitmead helped Father Redlich to pack his few possessions and the two men set off to find the refuge of Louis Austen, a retired sea-captain who managed a government coffee plantation near Sangara. After several hours' trekking, and helped by natives, they found his shelter and later were joined by two American airmen who had been shot down on a bombing mission.

That night the four men made plans. Harry Bitmead set out with the Americans to reach Port Moresby. Captain Austen had an ulcerated leg and was unfit to trek across country. Vivian Redlich would stay with him and his people and move among them. He wanted to find the two women from Sangara Mission and join other missionaries he knew were hiding in the jungle. He scribbled a last hasty note to his father, who received it from a Field Post Office.

Somewhere in the Papuan bush
July 27 1942

My dear Dad,

The war has busted up here. I got back from Dogura and ran right into it – and am now somewhere in my parish trying to carry on, though my people are horribly scared.

No news of May and I'm cut off from contacting her – my staff O.K. so far but in another spot. I'm trying to stick whatever happens. If I don't come out of it just rest content that I've tried to do my job faithfully.

Rush chance of getting word out, so forgive brevity.

God bless you all,

Vivian.

Vivian Redlich found the two women from Sangara Mission. He also located, in another part of the jungle, Henry Holland, a missionary, and John Duffill, a young mission builder, from the nearby Isivita Mission, some seven miles from Sangara. All of them were Australians. Along with Captain Austen the party found a hiding-place on the Upper Kumusi River.

Six weeks later this group tried to reach the coast, piloted by Lucian Tapiedi, a Papuan teacher-evangelist. They joined another party of refugees: Tony Gors who was Captain Austen's half-caste assistant, Gors's six year old son, and a young mixed-race woman, Louise Artango. They would have succeeded in eluding the Japanese but for the treachery of heathen Papuans who captured them as they were crossing a river. Tapiedi protested to their captors that the missionaries were 'good people in the country to help them'. He was struck dead with an axe by his fellow-Papuans, and then, anxious to ingratiate themselves with the invaders, they dragged the others to the Japanese at Buna. The man who killed him was later baptized, taking the Christian name of Lucian, and it was he who opened the door of the new church in Embi village when it was dedicated to St. Lucian Tapiedi in 1965.

On August 6, the Feast of the Transfiguration, they were all beheaded on the beach at Buna, the then headquarters of the Japanese Army. The six year old boy was killed last. Their bodies were thrown into the sea and were never recovered. The sorcerer and betrayer Embogi, made a 'captain' by the Japanese and given a white armband to denote his authority, was satisfied.

*

At Gona Mission Vivian's fiancée May Hayman, the nurse and housekeeper, had just put the dinner in the oven. She sat down with Mavis Parkinson, a fellow-Australian and a teacher, to tackle mending heaped on the dining-room table – khaki shirts and shorts left behind by young Australian soldiers. They had stopped at Gona the night before on their way to the wireless station at Ambasi.

Gona was the most beautiful place on the coast, a garden between beach and jungle. Behind a good-looking church of grey woven sago-leaf a school with reedy walls of sago-stalk stood close by a cricket field. The grounds were well-shaded by tulip trees and palms, and yellow crotons and red hibiscus bordered the paths.

Now its peace was shattered. As a preliminary to landings, the Japanese began bombardments of Gona at 4.45 p.m. on July 21, 1942. The ground shook with explosions and when the Mission staff saw Japanese transports put down dinghies and soldiers climb into them, they decided to move. Father James Benson, the white-haired English priest-in-charge, and May and Mavis flung some belongings into a box which Mission boys carried along the only road out of Gona. It was about 6.30, and already dark. They stopped at the first garden house along the track, said evensong with the boys, put up mosquito nets and prepared to settle down.

Suddenly they heard footsteps. The women called out, first in English, then in Motu, a kind of Papuan pidgin. A torch flashed. They saw the outline of a soldier and realized they had called to a Japanese patrol. Each grabbed a few things, crept away down to the track, and darted into the bush.

Fortunately they soon found each other and after James Benson had looked at his compass, turned north. They had not gone far when planes roared overhead in another raid on Gona which was bombed throughout the day at intervals of less than half-an-hour. The missionaries camped by a tree with a turkey nest at the foot. Next day, they waded into a sago swamp and had to retrace their steps. At last, they reached a clean running stream which refreshed them, and then, to their joy, met some friendly natives who prepared them food.

The party sent a message by the natives to Siai, a Mission outstation on the lower Kumusi River, asking Father John, a native priest, to meet them. The Siai people gave them food and hot water and clean clothes. The villagers built a hut for the missionaries deep in the bush where they could hide. It seemed safe enough until August 8 when rumours reached them that the Japanese were advancing. They moved on again. 'We cannot risk trouble for the natives if they're found hiding white people,' said Father Benson. They joined five Australians, five Americans and five Papuan soldiers, all of whom wanted to get to Port Moresby by making for Popondetta and crossing the saddle of Mount Lamington to reach the capital. They successfully slipped past the Japanese and were not far from Popondetta when firing started. A native guide had betrayed them and they were ambushed. According to plan, they scattered. Father Benson lost the women and the rest of the party. He prayed for their protection, and called softly from the bush to try to contact them.

About 9.00 the firing petered out and he thanked God, thinking the others had escaped. In fact, they did get away that night; but two days later were surrounded by hostile natives who delivered them to the Japanese. All but the two women and an Australian lieutenant, who managed to flee into the jungle, were killed. The two women became separated from the Australian, and again were betrayed by natives. The Japanese imprisoned them in a wire coffee store and taunted them with food withdrawn once the women stretched out a hand. Next day they were taken to a coffee plantation where a trench had been dug. Here they were murdered and buried.

*

The base of the coffee store still stands on Popondetta station beside the creek and upon it has been built the priest's house. The site of martyrdom is now marked by a stone altar standing in the bush beside the new main road to Oro Bay. Eucharist is celebrated there on Martyrs Day – September 2 – each year, as at other martyrdom sites in New Guinea.

A May Hayman memorial window was contributed to the church May attended while she was nursing in Canberra. In the hospital where she worked is a plaque and a bowl of fresh flowers kept to her memory.

The only one of the staff of two Mission stations to survive the war was James Benson. He suffered terrible ordeals, but after imprisonment in New Britain, was able to return to New Guinea.

One of the first requests for Christian teaching when missionary work was renewed in the Gona area came from the villages which had been ruled by Embogi, sorcerer and criminal. Amazingly, Embogi professed Christianity at the end. Captive and sentenced to death, he spoke from the scaffold to a crowd of his own Jegarata people. 'I have ruled you for many years and told you that the message of the Mission is wrong,' he said. 'However, I have now become a Christian myself and all my followers, except two, have been baptized. I want you now to ask the Mission to come to your village. Send your children to its schools. Learn about God in their churches . . .' And, still the autocrat, his last words were, 'I *command* you to go to the Mission.'

When news of Vivian's martyrdom became known, a young priest working near his old home in England was inspired to take his place in Papua. A series of coincidences linked the two priests. David Hand was serving his first curacy at Heckmondwike in the parish of Wakefield, neighbouring Dewsbury Moor. Although he joined the Mission from England, he was born in Queensland, Australia, and his father was rector of Clermont in the diocese of Rockhampton, where Redlich served as Bush Brother. Hand's father and Redlich's father had been ordained during the same ceremony at Lincoln Cathedral.

The diocese of Rockhampton established a Redlich Memorial Fund to train Papuan ordination candidates and named a new school at Rockhampton after him. The Diocesan Conference at Dogura Cathedral in 1947 discussed how they could best commemorate the martyrs. The Government had offered to build a school but there could be no guarantee of committed Christian teaching. If they wanted a school with religious instruction, they must build it and pay for it. They did; and a year later, the 'Martyrs' Memorial School' was dedicated by Bishop Strong.

In 1951 Mount Lamington erupted and Sangara was almost wiped out. About 4,000 people were killed or injured. The Mission and school lay in ruins. David Hand flew back from Australia and spent two years re-establishing the work at Popondetta, which was chosen to replace both Sangara as Mission head station and Higaturu, also destroyed, as Government headquarters.

The people came to Bishop David and said, 'We will build our new Church here and it will be called "Resurrection" to remind us that like its Master, the Church always rises again after disaster.' The original Resurrection Church was replaced by a permanent building in the late nineteen sixties and is now Resurrection Cathedral of Popondota Diocese. There is a move to bring back the correct Papuan name of *Popondota* but it is more widely known by its anglicized name of *Popondetta*. At present the town is called Popondetta and the new Diocese, Popondota. Sangara was restored as an outstation and the Martyrs' school rebuilt at Agenehambo which is five miles further along the Kokoda Road.

The year before the Lamington disaster – on St. Peter's Day, June 29, 1950 – David Hand had been chosen and consecrated as Assistant Bishop of the Diocese of New Guinea, which was then part of the Province of Queensland, and so became the youngest Anglican bishop in the world. He went to Australia for leave and a speaking tour. He was to be Bishop with special responsibility for starting Anglican work in the Trust Territory of New Guinea. This area was opened by the Australian Government to white people gradually as it was explored by Government patrols, and a census taken. The Australian Church promised staff and money for this enterprise and Bishop David was to lead it. The Lamington eruption and its aftermath delayed this project.

Bishop Strong left New Guinea to become Archbishop of Brisbane in 1963, and the same year David Hand was enthroned as the new Bishop of New Guinea.

Papua New Guinea, once annexed by Britain and later administered by Australia under mandate of the League of Nations (later the United Nations) became an independent nation in 1975. Two years later new status was given to the Diocesan Bishop, David Hand. He was enthroned as first Archbishop of the Province of Papua New Guinea. Dancers and drummers with painted faces, masks, and bird of paradise plumes, led the procession of bishops from Polynesia, Melanesia, Australia, and Papua New Guinea itself. The Archbishop of Canterbury, Dr. Donald Coggan, represented the rest of the Anglican Communion. The occasion was the first visit of any Archbishop of Canterbury to Papua New Guinea, which now has five Anglican bishops, over a hundred national priests and more than 150,000 Church members.

*

Morva Kekwick, mutual friend and fellow missionary in Papua, remembers both Vivian Redlich and May Hayman.

'May's offer to serve in this Diocese was born of a real desire to be of service to mankind. A warm-hearted champion of the defenceless, the weak and the "under-dogs" of the world, her efforts on their behalf were unfailing . . . Laughter, friendliness and generosity were all a part of May . . . Vivian and she were ideally suited.

'Vivian Redlich had a constant vision of the Risen Christ. I am confident that in those last dreadful days that vision must have been a strength and comfort to him and that he must in very truth have walked with our Lord.'

Daw Pwa Sein

1894–1942

Steadfast confession of the Christian faith is another face of martyrdom. The compulsion to witness is so urgent that silence can in some circumstances become to the Christian both strident denial of God and base disloyalty to him.

Daw Pwa Sein, Burmese headmistress, knew special responsibility as a Christian leader and was aware she would shirk this at her spiritual peril. To refuse to witness would destroy her credentials; she would become a lesser woman, perhaps even a different woman. She had to die to give continuing personal credence to her faith.

The bitterly hard decision involved the sacrifice of other lives; but she believed that love and sacrifice both triumph over death.

The settlement of Burma was determined even during the Stone Ages, tribes from the vast expanses of Central Asia coming from the North over the mountains and then down the great rivers. Of these people, the earlier or stronger settled in the valleys and the later weaker groups were pushed into the mountainous regions.

Among these hill tribes were the Karens, Kachins and Chins, less educated, less politically effective, more impoverished, than the Burmese of the plains.

The Karens, largest of these despised minorities, were originally animists but became Christians in increasing numbers since the beginning of the nineteenth century. They made valiant Christians, but in the eyes of the Burmese, the majority race, they were traitors to the national religion. And there was an innate hostility between Burmese and Karens which existed even before the coming of Christianity; it was born of the contempt of the stronger more sophisticated men of the plains towards the simple primitive people of the hills.

Another faction in Burma, feared by the whole population, are the 'dacoits', roving armed gangs, on the make. Dacoity, an Indian word for banditry, has been endemic in Burma for generations, both in peace and war. Dacoits, mostly Burmese, are opportunists, always ready to seize advantage of restless conditions for terrorism and gain. This brigandry may have begun because of the enforced idleness of a rice-producing people, without work once the grain was harvested. Dacoity was always worse in the hot weather months before the rains broke.

In the last war when Burma was invaded, many of the dacoits became agents of the Japanese. They saw in the general confusion of occupation, particularly in the transition between the British fighting retreat and the establishment of the new Japanese order, ideal conditions for their lawlessness.

They were hostile both to the British, whom they saw as oppressors of the Burmese, and the Karens because of their friendship with the British and Americans. They were also opposed to the Christians whose faith was shared by many of the Allies and the Karens.

The Christians in Burma had forged close ties with the Allies. This meant that both the Japanese and the nationalists suspected their loyalties. Once the Japanese had come it was dangerous to be known as friends of the British and Americans, who had given the country an alien religion – they also provided more than half of the country's schools – and were now at war with the Japanese. The Christian population numbered little more than half a million and of these only a small fraction belonged to the main race of Burmese. Yet the Christians' influence through education and spiritual leadership was disproportionate to their numbers.

In 1942 out of a population of nearly seventeen million, over ten million were Burmese and nearly all of these were Buddhists. Of the remainder the Karens were the largest of the groups, numbering 1,400,000. Shans accounted for a million, there were 400,000 Kachins, and 350,000 Chins. The Shans were Buddhists; but large numbers of the Karens, Kachins and Chins were becoming Christians, especially the Karens. Most vulnerable of all during the invasion were the Karen Christians.

*

Ma Pwa Sein (the child is called Ma; the mature woman Daw) was born in 1894, at Ohyone Quarter, Moulmein, one of the earliest British centres in south Burma and built near the place where the River Salween joins the Indian Ocean. She was born a Burmese and was brought up as a Buddhist. Moulmein was a strong American Baptist stronghold because the first successful missionary to Burma, the American Baptist, Dr. Adoniram Judson, who reached the country in 1813, had lived in the region and founded a Christian community.

Ma Pwa Sein's father taught at a boys' Mission School, St. Augustine's, but he was a staunch Buddhist. His new daughter was the child of a second marriage and Ma Pwa Sein had three half-brothers and a half-sister. Although in those days girls were not encouraged to attend school, he wanted his daughter to benefit from the modern education brought by the missionaries. So he sent her to St. Agnes Girls' School, which was in the same compound as St. Augustine's School and Church in Maunggan Quarter, about a mile's walk from their home.

But he was not in favour of her becoming a Christian. 'Work hard. Pay attention to your teachers, but do not listen to their religious instruction. You are a follower of Buddha,' he impressed upon her. She remembered his words and when one of her teachers, noticing her inattention, gave her a Bible, she tore it up.

The child loved to accompany her father to the long hill behind the old town which was crested with pagodas, the Buddhist spires dazzling white in the tropical sun. While her father made his devotions, Ma Pwa Sein was content watching all the people who came to pray and meditate. Most of all she liked to see a procession of the yellow-robed monks and to hear the deep echo of the monastery gong.

Then, as the years passed, she gradually determined, in spite of her strict Buddhist upbringing, to learn about the religion of her Christian school-friends. She finally resolved to become a Christian and to ask 'Mr. Pope', the English missionary in charge of the school where her father taught, to baptize her.

Mr. Pope was dismayed, because he knew there was a close bond of affection between the girl and her father, who was also his colleague and friend. 'It would cause great unhappiness at home,' he told the girl gently. 'I know, but I have made up my mind,' she replied. 'Go home and tell your father, and if you're still in earnest come to see me again,' he advised.

Ma Pwa Sein returned home dismayed at the thought of hurting her father. She wasted no time but summoned her courage and faced him. 'If you follow the Christian religion, I shall turn you out of my house,' her father said firmly. She was fourteen years old.

Her father's sternness was mingled with sadness, and self-recrimination. Education was not everything; Ma Pwa Sein was young and impressionable; but the fault was his for sending her to a Christian school. Religion in a good mission school pervaded the whole atmosphere, spilling over into every department. His daughter was a Burmese and all good Burmese revered Gautama, the Buddha.

The Buddhist looked at his young daughter with new eyes. The obedient small child who had played on the Ridge of the Pagodas while he listened to the *pongyi* (monk) teaching the Buddhist law, had changed, grown up, almost overnight it seemed. He knew his own child; this was not a whim, a wish to copy Christian schoolfriends, but a stubbornness born of conviction. 'You're making a mistake,' he said in a low voice. 'Don't do it.' It was a command, and an entreaty. By changing her faith she was relinquishing more than a child of her years could imagine. She was giving up the safety net of national loyalties, which her father may intuitively have known would become increasingly important in her lifetime.

Three months later Ma Pwa Sein reappeared at St. Augustine's and told the missionary she still wanted to become a Christian despite her father's warnings. 'Why not wait until you are a little older?' demurred Mr. Pope. He liked and respected the Buddhist teacher and disliked the idea of precipitating a quarrel which would divide the family.

The child was more than a match for him. She said resolutely, 'I came to you because you are my father's friend, but if you will not christen me, I shall go to the Baptists. They will!'

Mr. Pope gave in. 'Come to me every week and I will prepare you.' After some weeks the girl stood at the font in St. Augustine's Church and was christened. That day when she went home she found herself locked out. She returned to Mr. Pope a homeless child; she had called her father's bluff. The missionaries sent her back as a boarder to St. Agnes.

The girl missed her father and prayed that he might relent of his harshness in disowning her. One day some time later she saw him walking along the road. He was with a friend and appeared not to notice her. She smiled tentatively and strained her ears, only to hear the friend remark, 'Isn't that your daughter?' and her father reply curtly, 'No child of mine.'

Eventually the Buddhist teacher was reconciled with his young Christian daughter. Ma Pwa Sein was ill at the Mission House and Mr. Pope's sister, who was nursing her, feared she had smallpox. Her father was sent for urgently. He came and diagnosed chicken-pox. He was correct, but the child was very ill and he visited her again. So the breach was healed at the sick-bed. When Ma Pwa Sein was well enough, her father took her home to convalesce, and now she was welcome again in the school holidays. 'But I don't want to hear anything about your new religion,' he warned her.

When her father turned Ma Pwa Sein out of his house, Daw Susan, an unmarried teacher at her school, had befriended the girl. Soon afterwards Daw Susan married the Rev. U. San Nyunt and they moved nearer Rangoon. But their friendship was valued by Ma Pwa Sein and she kept in touch with her 'foster parents' and visited them often, particularly after her father's death. He died during her course at the Teachers' Training School run by the American Baptists in Morton Lane, Moulmein. It was hard for her to hold apart from the Buddhist rites. Her father was an obdurate man – she had inherited her own stubbornness from him – but she had loved him. More and more she was to understand his fatherly concern, as well as his anger, at her conversion to Christianity.

*

As soon as she qualified Daw Pwa Sein was sent to St. Mary's at Kemmendine, some four miles north of Rangoon. The School was known as the Normal Teachers' Training School with a Practising School attached, and she was to teach there for more than thirty years, rapidly becoming Headmistress, with one of the Christian women missionaries acting as Principal.

The Normal School ran two courses: one for training secondary schoolteachers took about fifty students and lasted two years; the other for teaching juniors ran only one year and trained half that number. Students from both sections gained teaching experience in the Practising School adjoining, which had 100–150 pupils.

St. Mary's mainly served South Burma, with many Karen girls from the villages of the Irrawaddy Delta which covered a large

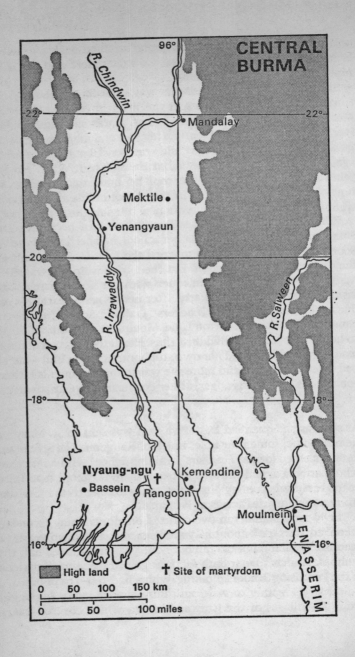

CENTRAL BURMA

R. Chindwin

96°

22°   22°
                    ● Mandalay

                Mektile ●

                ● Yenangyaun

20°

R. Irrawaddy

R. Salween

18°   18°

            Nyaung-ngu   †
            ● Bassein   Kemendine ●
                        Rangoon

                            Moulmein ●

16°   16°
                                        T
                                        E
      High land   † Site of martyrdom   N
                                             A
   0   50   100   150 km   S
                                             S
   0   50   100 miles   E
                                             R
                                             I
                                             M

area some 80–100 miles west and south of Rangoon. But under Daw Pwa Sein's leadership the school enhanced its reputation and began to attract pupils from all parts of Burma. Soon there was a waiting-list and every year many applicants had to be refused.

Women in Burma have always enjoyed equal rights with men and Daw Pwa Sein grew into a woman of considerable authority and influence. She had personal magnetism and was highly regarded by both Christians and non-Christians. She also had a name for being a strict headmistress; she would not tolerate bad behaviour or any falling short of Christian standards. Daw Pwa Sein taught in a simple direct style, secular subjects on weekdays – history was her specialism – and religious education on Sundays.

The girls respected her and there were few disciplinary problems at St. Mary's. It is also no exaggeration to say they loved her, because although strict she was always approachable. They could talk to her about any of their troubles.

The students also admired her elegance. She was a small woman, always neat and prettily dressed in a colourful *long-gyi* (the long tubular skirt worn by both men and women, which wraps around and tucks into the waist), muslin blouse, pert sandals. Her gleaming black hair would be coiled into traditional flowerpot shape, the *s'done*, and as is the habit, she and her staff made up their faces by putting on a paste of *thanakha*, the ground bark of a tree. This made them feel and look cooler by absorbing perspiration.

Daw Pwa Sein showed special warmth to any orphan girls at St. Mary's because she never forgot her own desolation when disowned by her Buddhist father. Often she would stay at the School during the holidays with the orphans, or she would take them with her visiting friends. The Mission may have assumed responsibility for them but it was Daw Pwa Sein who mothered them and gave them holidays to remember. Her ideal holiday was to travel around the country looking up her 'old girls'. They were scattered throughout Burma, and, Christian or Buddhist, she remembered each of them.

St. Mary's campus was green and pleasant, planted with traditional English flowers as well as blazing with the indigenous flowering trees, the gold mohur and the sweet-scented frangipani. It provided a peaceful background for study, and the huge slatted wooden shutters protected the girls from the heat of the sun.

Before sunrise on December 7, 1941, a Japanese naval force made a shattering attack on Pearl Harbor, the American naval base in the Hawaiian Islands. President Roosevelt described it as 'a date which will go down in infamy'. In under an hour the Japanese gained control of the Pacific. The way was cleared by this single stroke for the seaborne invasion of American, British and Dutch territories in that ocean. Simultaneously with the bombing of Pearl Harbor, landings began in the Malay Peninsula, and there were air raids on Singapore, the great British naval base which was considered an impregnable fortress.

As the war clouds gathered over the Far East, it was decided that St. Mary's, Kemmendine, should be evacuated. Daw Pwa Sein, with some of her staff and those girls who wished to continue their studies, moved to the small Karen village of Nyaung-ngu in the Delta. They packed their personal belongings, bed-rolls and books, and made the eleven hours' journey by river steamer. The party was welcomed by the small community of Karen Christians and they 'camped' in the S.P.G. Mission, simple buildings of wood and bamboo standing on stilts beside the river-bank amid the banana groves.

The Japanese invasion of Burma had actually started as early as mid-December when a detachment of their 15th Army moved in to Tenasserim, on the Burmese side of the Kra Isthmus, to seize the three key airfields there and so block the route for British air reinforcements to Malaya.

Rangoon, capital city and principal port in the country, was bombed at Christmas. The bombs, 50- and 100-pounders, were intended to kill rather than systematically destroy buildings, and two thousand died in one day. As the Indian labour force fled, and refugees blocked roads, the life of the city was reduced to chaos. The port became semi-paralysed.

Under cover of widespread confusion, the dacoits added their own brand of terror, plundering the devastated city. Their most frequent crime was to pilfer arms from the Allied military stores.

*

Iris Miller was Principal at St. Mary's when the war came to Burma. She accompanied the headmistress, Daw Pwa Sein, and other teachers when the School was evacuated to the Delta, where they tried to make conditions as normal as possible for the girls to continue their studies.

One day soon after the evacuation, Daw Pwa Sein and Iris Miller went to Rangoon to buy a trousseau for Ivy, one of the orphan girls. Ivy was to marry the son of one of the friends of the headmistress with whom she spent many holidays. The shops were already short of cloth, but they managed to buy the excited girl some pretty clothes and saw her off at the railway station to join the bridegroom's family.

But what had started as a happy outing had a dismal sequel. The two women stayed at Kemmendine, where domestic staff were looking after the school, and Iris was told by the Rev. Hugh Wilson, the Bishop's Commissary, that she must not return to the Delta because plans were already under way for the evacuation of European women mission workers from the area. Tears filled her eyes as she said goodbye to Daw Pwa Sein. For eight years she had worked alongside her. She hated to see Daw Pwa Sein return alone to the Karen village. 'I feel I failed her,' she said years later. Iris was put aboard a troopship for Calcutta.

*

On February 1, 1942, a small conclave of priests and teachers sat cross-legged on the bamboo floor of the Mission at Nyaung-ngu. The war news had worsened and they met to make emergency plans to face the Occupation. The Japanese had crossed the frontier from Thailand and captured Moulmein, only 130 miles southeast of the capital, after a stiff battle on January 31.

Singapore, which had been garrisoned by 20,000 men, had surrendered on February 15, four days before the missionaries had their crisis meeting. The Japanese used bicycles, not troopships. Singapore defences faced mainly seaward, and the jungle, which had been expected to defend the place from the landward side, did not impede the Japanese. They walked, they bicycled, they did not need roads.

Burma had become a battlefield with Commonwealth troops fighting a grim retreat of a thousand miles all the way back to India.

What should the missionaries do? The Rev. George Appleton,

Warden of Holy Cross Theological College, Rangoon (later to become Archdeacon of Rangoon, then Archbishop of Perth, Western Australia, and finally Archbishop in Jerusalem) said that the men missionaries were prepared to stay.

The Burmese had reservations. Daw Pwa Sein was emphatic that the English should not fall into the hands of the Japanese. The headmistress urged that they should withdraw to safety to be free to return as soon as possible. Others were apprehensive that the presence of Westerners would draw dangerous attention to their villages. The Japanese were at war with the British not the Burmese.

Saya Own Bwint, the senior Karen priest present, relieved the tension with a shaft of humour. He glanced at George Appleton and said wryly, 'We could dress you in Burmese clothes, we could darken your skin and dye your hair. You speak Burmese well enough. But we could do nothing with that English nose!' It was decided that the missionaries should move to Upper Burma.

George Appleton tried to prepare the village churches to adapt to the realities of the Occupation. They would be cut off from any fellowship with the Church outside and there would be no S.P.G. grants. After paying school salaries he left them £150. When the money ran out the keep of the clergy was to be the first charge on all church offerings. The priests would work in the fields if necessary. The meeting then learnt that supplies of wafers and wine for Holy Communion were nearly exhausted and decided that grains of boiled rice would substitute for the wafers; and tea, water, or coconut milk replace the wine.

Daw Pwa Sein insisted that the students must be taken home and men teachers from the local school were deputed to conduct the Delta girls to their home villages. Only a few orphaned schoolgirls without homes would stay on at Nyaung-ngu with Daw Pwa Sein and several of her colleagues. It was a small village away from the main lines of communication and was unlikely to be in danger from the advancing Japanese.

George Appleton undertook to escort the girls who lived beyond Rangoon when he returned to the city on the night steamer. When his party, which included an English missionary nurse, and a group of Burmese students, pulled out in sampans and canoes to board a crowded boat waiting in mid-stream, it was already dark. From the shadows figures on the river bank waved lanterns and called farewells and blessings. The steamer docked at Rangoon in the early morning to find that civil evacuation had been ordered, and the quays were crowded with frightened refugees.

The next day all the Mission's workers left Rangoon for the north. Three weeks later General Sir Harold Alexander ordered the military evacuation of the capital, after demolitions on March 7. To their surprise the Japanese occupied a deserted city on the 8th.

During the two months between the fall of Rangoon and their flight to India, mission workers turned to relief work. Women missionaries drove ambulances and helped in the Forces' canteens; priests worked in hospital laundries and scrubbed blood-stained floors. Several enrolled as chaplains. They fought fires, looked after refugees, organized the evacuation of large crowds; but they never thought that they would have to evacuate Burma completely.

*

An early directive issued to the Japanese occupying forces told them 'to respect the opinions of the natives and to take a true, fatherly attitude towards them'. The Japanese schemed to promote anti-colonist feelings and to present themselves in the heroic role of liberators rather than invaders. They proclaimed a programme to increase nationalist awareness and to hasten independence, but the independence they gave was more symbolic than real for it took the form of a puppet Government. They also made the most of the fact that they were fellow-Asians, with the same religion as the Buddhists.

But for all their propaganda about a common goal of a more prosperous Greater East Asia, it soon became apparent that the Japanese saw the Burmese as slaves to advance their war effort. They boasted to other occupied countries that they had made them 'into one vast sweat army'. The Japanese introduced Fascist controls. All radio sets were called in and altered to receive only Japanese wave-lengths. Christians were not allowed to meet for corporate worship, except for a few native groups among the Baptists; and in the towns, churches were requisitioned as storehouses, stables and factories, and all the furniture and fittings looted.

As the Japanese advanced up-country, stories spread of atrocities and forced recantations. At Shwebo, in Central Burma, an attempt was made by Japanese and their Burmese collaborators to stamp out the Christian religion. Peter Ba Shin was singled out for torture as the latest Christian convert; his persecutors hoped that if he recanted, others would follow. But Peter lived up to his name, stayed firm as a rock, and the attempt was abandoned.

Despite a Japanese census of all Christians in some areas, and the disapproval of the *Kempathai* (Japanese military police), many courageous priests held regular services in private houses. They trekked miles and bicycled up and down the hills to minister to their people in lonely villages. One priest went to Ba Maw, the Burmese Dictator, and asked that Christian churches should be handed back for worship. Another, suspected of being pro-British, was hung by his feet from the rafters of his house with a fire lit beneath him. He endured patiently, and the Japanese officer was moved to spare his life when he was led out for execution. Education practically stopped, although in many Christian villages the teachers carried on without salaries, helped by contributions in kind from parents.

Economically, Burma was ruined, for it depended on its exports – rice, oil, teak, silver, lead and tungsten – for prosperity. Everything was short – food, cloth, medicines, soap. These shortages were to get worse as the communications of the country were disrupted by Allied bombing and machine-gunning of trains, boats and bullock-carts, and by Japanese slaughter of draught cattle for food. The movement of such boats and carts as were left was restricted because of attacks by dacoits.

Many dacoits formed an alliance with the Japanese because they believed they might profit from such an arrangement. The invaders were also welcomed by extreme nationalists who saw the Japanese as liberators from the British. But the majority of the people simply acquiesced in the Occupation. Large numbers of villagers did not know what was going on. They just wanted to be left in peace and to grow their rice and get a good price for it.

*

Early in April 1942 a strengthened Japanese 15th Army moved north up the Irrawaddy towards Mandalay, to close the Burma supply road to China. The British, some 60,000 strong, were holding a line 150 miles south of Mandalay, helped by Chinese forces on their eastern flank. But the Japanese moved round their western flank, enveloping the defenders and capturing the Yenangyaung oilfields. General Alexander decided not to make a stand at Mandalay but to make a fighting withdrawal to the Indian frontier and the borders of Assam before the mid-May monsoon flooded rivers and roads. His troops succeeded in delaying the Japanese advance until the rains came and so saved India from invasion.

The Japanese pushed up the Chindwin River to cut off the British retreat and nearly succeeded. As it was, all the British tanks were lost but most of the soldiers got away before the rains. Even so, British casualties were treble those of the Japanese.

In the first week of June some stragglers from the British Army, who had hopelessly lost their way in the heavy rains, arrived in Nyaung-ngu, their eyes red-rimmed from fatigue, their feet blistered from wet boots. They had colic and diarrhoea.

Daw Pwa Sein and her fellow Christians gave them food and shelter, washed their feet and attended their ills. Soon the soldiers were fit to leave. Daw Pwa Sein told them their safest route to link up with the Army in the north. She also cautioned them, 'Take great care. You must move secretly because there is a large armed band of dacoits in the district. They're anti-British, many of them are agents for the Japanese.'

'Dacoits? Who are the *dacoits*? What in Christ's name – begging your pardon Ma'am – have they got against us?' The soldiers had only recently landed in Burma and knew next to nothing about the people or the country. They couldn't tell the difference between Burmese, Chinese, Japanese and Gurkhas. Now *dacoits*! They were a new threat.

'They are bandits,' explained the headmistress, 'and they are making the most of the war. They're Burmese, but remember, they're against the British.'

The soldiers swore softly. What a Goddam awful war! It seemed to them that most of the people they were fighting to defend were against them. 'That doesn't surprise us,' said one young soldier wearily. 'Do you know we've actually been fired on by people who look like monks,'

Daw Pwa Sein looked at them with pity. She said, 'It's a common Japanese trick to disguise themselves as Buddhist monks. You must not trust your eyes. But believe me, most of the people of Burma are your friends.'

The British troops were fighting a campaign for which they were ill-prepared, and under strength. Britain, helping hard-pressed Russia as well as fighting for her own survival, was unable to send enough men or machines for Burma's defence. The soldiers were untrained in jungle warfare and kept largely to the roads. At one point the evacuation column stretched for seventy miles.

Daw Pwa Sein wished the soldiers godspeed, and brushed aside their thanks. 'It was nothing.' Almost as an afterthought – she knew that reprisals for helping the Allies were commonplace – she added, 'Don't tell anyone we sheltered you.'

Everyone imagined that the Christian community would be safe enough in the Irrawaddy Delta, for the Japanese made only occasional raids on the villages to commandeer food and impress labour. But in June a large armed mob of dacoits struck through the Delta and made Nyaung-ngu, the S.P.G. Centre, one target for vicious attack.

Early in the morning of June 5, the Karen village was surprised by an angry band, each armed with a *dah* – the knife that every man carries to chop bamboo, behead chickens and fulfil all manner of everyday domestic purposes. They had heard that the Christians had sheltered some British soldiers.

'Bring out all the Karen Christians,' ordered one of the dacoits. Daw Pwa Sein watched the Christian Karens gather in a terrified group. She did not hesitate but turned to her teachers and students. 'We are not Karens,' she said, 'but we are Christians and we must stand by them.' Her mind was made up. She was the leader of the Christian community; she could not take advantage of the fact that she was a Burmese, not a Karen, to save her own life. Her fellow Christians were in peril.

She joined the group, followed by the others, and stood in front of the Karens. A slight figure, with poise and elegance, she was no match for their violent adversaries. But her spiritual stature was great.

'You have been helping British soldiers,' shouted one of the dacoits. 'You shall die!' The band of robbers were stony-faced, unmoved by pleas, inured to killing, even women and children. She knew they meant their words. Daw Pwa Sein asked for a few minutes to pray with her three teachers and four schoolgirls. They were Daw Thit, Daw Sein Thit, and Daw Aye Nyein, teachers of St. Mary's, Kemmendine; and schoolgirls, Hilda, Ann, Ma Tin Shwe and Naw Pi Pi, a Karen girl.

Swiftly they were hacked to pieces. Some sixty Christians were murdered in this small massacre in the Delta, most of them Karens as well as Christians.

*

'Switch On!' The order rang out loud and clear, and Rangoon Cathedral was dramatically lit by twenty jeeps lined up outside and playing their beams through the windows. The electricity supply for the city was still erratic so the lighting for the momentous Service of Thanksgiving for Victory, on July 2, 1945, was by courtesy of the military. One jeep drove into the Cathedral and from the west end its headlamps blazed so that all could read the service sheets.

Two days earlier there had been a Service of Reconciliation when the great Cathedral filled with members of the three Services – called by Winston Churchill 'The Great Forgotten Army' – and Burmese Christians. The service was based on mediaeval rites for the re-hallowing of desecrated churches, for the Japanese had used the Cathedral to distil *saki* (toddy). The brick-built vats in which the spirit had been distilled had occupied the nave. The rest of the Cathedral was used as a cattle shed at night and overflow from the vats and cow-dung once covered the marble floor. The Cathedral garden was a rubbish dump where the cattle 'grazed' by day. British and Indian soldiers, helped by Burmese Christians, set about reclamation. The whole place was filthy and the smell indescribable. The only bonus was finding the stained glass intact. The windows had been covered up by the British in 1941 as a protection against blast in Japanese air-raids, and when they took down the wood they found the glass undamaged. A detachment of Sikhs made pews and a new high altar from Burmese teak. Eventually the Cathedral was ready for worshippers.

The Reconciliation Service was taken by Bishop George West (Bishop of Rangoon 1935–1954) who had been in America during the Occupation, recovering from a motor accident. The cross-bearer was from the R.A.F., and the two servers from the Army and Navy.

Among the servicemen were representatives of Orde Wingate's jungle fighters, the Chindits. Wingate adopted this name after a mythical beast, the Chinthe, half-lion and half-eagle, his imagination caught by the way this creature symbolized the ground and air co-operation needed in jungle operations. Wingate's first expedition had been in February 1943 when the Chindits made sorties behind enemy lines. They attacked Japanese outposts, cut the railway in seventy places, blew up bridges and created ambushes. They kept in touch with their base by wireless and were supplied by air.

Within two months the Japanese counter-attacked strongly and the Chindits were back in India, having lost a thousand men and most of their equipment. But the campaign paid off. It proved that British and Indian troops could be effective jungle fighters. It raised morale by demonstrating that most Burmese were friendly; and convinced Japanese generals that the Chindwin River was not a defensive shield and they would have to advance to forestall a British counter-offensive. The repulse at Imphal of the Japanese offensive in the spring of 1944 saw the beginning of the liberation of Burma. The two main plans were 'Operation Capital', an overland thrust to recapture north central Burma, and 'Operation Dracula', an amphibious one to take south Burma.

Operation Dracula was launched with a parachute landing at the mouth of the Rangoon River and amphibious landings on both banks south of Rangoon. The troops moved rapidly up-river and on May 4 the capital was liberated.

Throughout the Occupation the clergy and individual Christians had remained loyal to their faith. Now in the refurbished Cathedral the English bishop headed a procession of Burmese clergy from the west end to the Sanctuary. Bishop West stopped at intervals to pray for the restoration of the Cathedral to the service of God, and sprinkled holy water on building and people alike. The huge congregation sang the hymn, 'We love the place, O God, Wherein thine honour dwells . . .' and the service ended with the glorious singing of the Te Deum, 'We Praise Thee O God, We acknowledge Thee to be the Lord, All the earth doth worship Thee, the Father Everlasting . . . O Lord, in Thee have I trusted.'

*

Seven months later Bishop George West and his wife, Grace, with a party of Christians from Rangoon, went by boat to the Delta Conference. On the return journey they stopped at Nyaung-ngu, pulling ashore in a rowing boat because the landing-stage no longer existed. They walked along the river-bank to the former site of the Mission where now flourished a large vegetable garden.

By the pathway nearby was a communal grave with a plain wooden cross five feet high, and carved on it the names of Daw Pwa Sein, her three fellow-teachers, and the four school-girls. A simple service was held by the grave, cordoned by young lime trees. Bishop West again led the singing of the Te Deum in thankfulness for victorious Christian lives. Among those who joined him, profoundly moved by their homage, was a young Karen priest, the Rev. Maung Kwai, who was the brother of Naw Pi Pi, the Karen girl slaughtered with the others.

The martyrdom of Daw Pwa Sein and her companions gave new blood to the Church. The dacoits themselves were influenced by her heroic constancy, and it was known that some became Christians. After the death of the Karen girl, Naw Pi Pi, her parents and the rest of her family became Christians. A staunch Buddhist became baptized and then confirmed, because he had seen some Christians die for their faith in Nyaung-ngu. 'The faith for which they died is the faith by which I wish to live,' he told the Bishop.

Roger Youderian

1924–1956

Roger Youderian, American missionary, and Toña, first Auca Indian missionary, both became disciples in the style of the early apostolic Church. Constantly in Roger's mind was Christ's promise to bequeath to the apostles the power of the Holy Spirit ... 'And ye shall be witnesses unto me ... unto the uttermost parts of the earth.' The words seized his imagination and spirit of adventure. Toña's life was evidence of the same convictions.

True discipleship dares all, and is buoyed by the implicit belief in the victorious power of love so strong that resort to violence, even in self-defence, is impossible. This does not mean that Christian lives should be jeopardized foolishly. Roger Youderian and his companions, and their wives, all prayed for God's protection. The women realized later that their prayers were granted and their men while on the most dangerous of expeditions had been shielded from disobedience to his will.

The Air Force Major was glad of the need to lower his gaze and escape the eyes of the five women who waited on his words. His face showed fatigue and strain as he frowned over his notebook. They had persuaded him it was unnecessary to soften the blow. They wanted to know everything.

He read in staccato sentences details of the bodies found in the Curaray, the river which writhed like a brown snake through the eastern jungle of Ecuador inhabited by the Auca Indians.

The Aucas were militantly inhospitable and had for many years challenged missionaries, endangered explorers, and embarrassed the Republic. Neighbouring tribes had named them 'Aucas', which means savage, barbarian.

A newsflash now informed the world, 'Five Men Missing in Auca Territory.'

The body of one of the American missionaries was found by some Quichua Indians. The U.S Army, Air Force and Navy continued to search with the government and military services of Ecuador for survivors, and thousands of people in all parts of the world prayed for their rescue. An army helicopter located the bodies of another four men floating in the river Curaray. Identification could not be positive until the corpses were recovered.

The Major reported sketchily, 'One body was caught under the branches of a fallen tree; only a large foot with a grey sock was visible at the surface of the muddy water ... Another had a red belt made from some woven material ... One had a tee-shirt and blue jeans ...'

He left the room silently, relieved yet disconcerted by the composure of the young widows. The large house at Shell Mera where they had gathered was on the fringe of the Jungle. It was the base for operations of Missionary Aviation Fellowship, an international transport organization for missionaries. It was also the home of Nate Saint, an M.A.F. pilot, and his wife, Marjorie. The women listened to the Major's report in Marj's bedroom to be away from the children playing unconcernedly.

Tee-shirt and blue jeans ... For one of the women the death of her husband, 32 years old, had been confirmed by Major Malcolm Nurnberg. The usual uniform of the men was white tee-shirt and khaki shorts. Roger Youderian was the only one who wore jeans.

Ironically, when Roger was asked at the eleventh hour if he would be fifth man for 'Operation Auca', to land the M.A.F. light plane on a sandbar in the heart of the Aucas country and pitch camp, he had been on the verge of quitting his vocation. He wrote in his diary, 'Failure to measure up as a missionary ... You can have my boots any time you want them.' But he had fought his way out of the spiritual crisis – 'my Waterloo as a missionary'. He joined the expedition to the Aucas gladly and expectantly.

His widow, Barbara, left with two young children, Beth Elaine, three and a half, and Jerry Lee, nearly two, wrote in her diary on the night she realized her husband was dead, January 12, 1956, 'I am sure this is the perfect will of God. I want to be free of self-pity. It is a tool of Satan to rot away a life ...'

*

Roger Youderian, paratrooper, aged 21, was a survivor of the Rhine jump and had been decorated for his service in the Battle of the Bulge. In August 1945 he wrote to his mother from Berlin.

'I've a secret to tell you,' the letter said. 'I've felt the call to either missionary, social, or ministerial work after my release from the Service ... Can't say now what the calling will be but I want to be a witness for him and live following him every second of my life.'

Roger dated his call to missionary work to a service held in Berlin that summer when the army chaplain preached from Matthew 9: 36 to 38, 'When Jesus saw the multitudes, he was moved with compassion on them, because they fainted, and were scattered abroad, as sheep having no shepherd. Then saith he unto his disciples, "The harvest truly is plenteous, but the labourers are few ..." '

Roger was the seventh and last child of a ranching family in Sumatra, Montana, and his mother was overjoyed to learn his secret because she had given all the children a strong Christian upbringing.

As she read the letter, she saw the resolution in her youngest son's deep set eyes. Roger was striking in appearance, tall, slim; thick black hair framing powerful features. He exuded a restless energy and a real sense of urgency. His mother knew him to have grown into a man of obdurate will who did not lightly give up or turn his back on a decision. He had a tenacity of purpose to achieve those goals which he set for himself. But he also demonstrated a gentle concern for the sick and disabled, born of his own suffering in childhood.

When he was nine he was stricken with polio, a special blow because it deprived him of his touch as a gifted pianist. Roger determined to overcome the crippling effects and at High School in Lewistown, Montana, he played basket-ball. Academically, he was a high flyer too. He planned to become a teacher in agriculture and he graduated from the Fergus County High School in Lewistown in 1941 with three scholarships. The next year he was named the outstanding freshman of his year at Montana State College where he started to study agriculture. His reward was a trip to the Youth Foundation Camp in Michigan in the summer of 1942. Later that year he worked for a land company, drawing some outstanding maps of farms around Lewistown which are still in use by the Federal Land Bank.

In October 1943 Roger enlisted in the Army, believing that if he went into military service his married brothers might not be

called up. Eventually he succeeded in joining the paratroopers –
although he had to learn to land on his hip and side because his
legs would not stand the shock of landing on his feet – and was
stationed in England.

During his time in the Army his faith deepened. His chaplain,
Paschal Fowlkes, wrote to his parents, 'Christian work in the
Army is not greatly different from Christian work outside . . . The
leader must learn to depend on a comparatively small number to
carry the load . . . I thought you would be happy to know that I
count Roger one of those "strong pillars".'

Upon demobilization, he was convinced he had a summons to
the mission field and he enrolled in the College of Liberal Art at
Northwestern Schools in Minneapolis, Minnesota. Here he met his
future wife and co-worker, Barbara Orton, a diffident, fair-haired
girl who was also studying Christian education with the mission
field her goal. Her background made her ideally suited for her
vocation. She came from a Baptist family in Lansing, Michigan,
and all her childhood she had become familiar with mission work.
Missionaries spoke at her church and she met them in her home. 'I
believe that the Lord spoke to me while I was a child and made me
feel that was what I should do,' she said simply.

In 1950 Roger and Barbara enrolled in the missionary medicine
course at Northwestern Schools, and learnt to deliver babies, set
bones and give injections. There followed in 1951 a course of
study at the Summer Institute of Linguistics at Norman, Okla-
homa, and that autumn they married. Both were accepted as candidates by the Gospel Missionary Union, a non-denominational
board, and they left at once for probationary work in Kansas City.
Here they studied Spanish, took turns leading Sunday services,
worked with children from the slums, and tackled some of the
practical problems of a mission station.

In January 1953 Roger and Betty, with their six months-old
daughter, Beth, set out for Ecuador. Letters written home from
Macuma by senior missionaries, Frank and Marie Drown, of Iowa,
had aroused Roger's desire to work among the Jivaros, the Indian
tribe famous for the ancient practice of shrinking human heads,
who live in the south eastern jungles.

The family made their home at the Macuma jungle station and
they immersed themselves in the task of learning the language of

the Jivaros. Soon, by an adaptation of the 'look and say' method of teaching children combined with phonetics, they were teaching the Indians to read and write their own tongue. Roger drew pictures of familiar jungle sights – a lizard lounging on a tree trunk, a sloth hanging upside down on a branch, a blow gun – and next to the pen and ink sketches he printed the sound of the Jivaro words.

A practical man, Roger was in his element. He liked to work with his hands and there was plenty to do in a jungle outpost. Roofs leaked from tropical rainstorms, generators broke down, and the rapid growth of the jungle had to be continually checked with the machete. He gloried in the noise of his power saw and the hard physical exertion.

In his mind God's word whispered. It had brought him to the Oriente, this remote and perilous territory on the far side of the Andes. Soon he spent most of his time visiting the homes of the Jivaros who lived throughout the seven thousand square miles of the southern jungle. It was risky, far removed from parish visiting! Dressed in tee-shirt, shorts, cotton cap and canvas leggings, he searched for his 'parishioners' down twisting overgrown tracks, often knee-high in mud and imperilled by snakes whose colouring provided insidious camouflage. He had to beware of the bushmaster, with enough poison in its sacs to kill a hundred men, and, even more treacherous, the small coral snake whose venom attacks the central nervous system and can bring death without warning symptoms within twenty-four hours. Another danger came from the traps the Indians often laid for their enemies; you could easily pierce your foot on one of the palm-wood spikes hidden along the trails that led to the Jivaros' houses. These were built like fortresses. They were oblong, thirty foot long, and had slits for windows. Each stood in its own clearing and the palm-thatched roof swept down to the ground. Inside a number of fires burnt at intervals on the earth floor, and filled the place with acrid smoke.

The men, who dressed their waist-long hair with the brilliant plumage of tropical birds, had their quarters at the front of the house, known as the *tangamash* and resembling the small front-porch of many houses in the small towns of the U.S.A. The women lived in the back of the house. Men had several wives and women were their chattels, often stolen or bartered.

Among the Jivaros, witchcraft and sorcery, hatred and murder, were concepts implanted in early childhood. Tribal killings and family feuds were routine. On going to sleep children were made to recite the names of those they must learn to hate. Roger spent hours talking to the Jivaros, familiarizing himself with their language and lifestyle. He told them about the life of Christ and worked to replace the children's bed-time 'hate list' with a prayer-roll for loved ones.

It was hard trying to combat the Jivaros' religion of fear and evil spirits, but Macuma was an established compound with an atmosphere of stability and permanence, thanks to Frank Drown who had run it since 1945. The work would go on. Roger began to pray for opportunities to extend the frontiers. In imitation of Paul the Apostle, he wrote passionately, 'It is my ambition to preach the Gospel, not where Christ has already been named . . .'

*

The Atshuaras, cousins but sworn enemies of the Jivaros, were among the tribes who had never heard of Christ. Five years earlier Frank Drown and another missionary had made overtures, but they had been repulsed on the threshold of the chief's house with the warning, 'Turn around or you'll be killed.' The tribe were fiercely suspicious of strangers and on tense terms with their neighbours.

On 5 June, 1954, Roger, challenged by their isolation as well as their ignorance of God, decided to move closer to the Atshuaras. For two days he slogged on foot to Wambimi, which he envisaged as the potential gateway settlement for work among the tribe. Here the Shell Oil Company had abandoned an airstrip and left several derelict houses. He tamed the grass with his machete and the airstrip was soon ready for Nate Saint's 'Piper Cruiser' to land. Nate flew in Barbara and the children and they set up home. Roger and Barbara began language study among the local Jivaros as well as their evangelistic work.

Most importantly, Roger carried on his medical ministry and this gave him his breakthrough. One of the diseases most alarming to the Indians was leishmaniasis, a sickness that is prolonged and disfiguring and ultimately kills. Roger tried a drug called 'repro-dral' and achieved two cures among the local Jivaros. Despite the perpetual feuding between the Jivaros and Atshuaras, as well as within both tribes, there was a grape-vine along the trail and news of his success soon spread. One of the chiefs of the Atshuaras, who was stricken with leishmaniasis, presented himself at Wambimi for treatment, the foreigner's 'magic'. Happily, the drug worked and the chief in jubilation invited Roger to his house. Roger was prudent enough to ask for an escort, before three of them, Frank Drown, another missionary, and himself, ventured into Atshuara-land.

Chief Sakitaku's house was enormous. You could have lost a basketball floor inside. The Atshuaras speak a dialect different from Jivaro but they understand this tongue, and for three days they sat listening to the story of Christ told them by the missionaries, helped by Gospel recordings made on a wind-up gramophone.

Before they left Frank Drown proposed to the Atshuaras that they should build an airstrip. Their isolation and enmity with their neighbouring cousins suggested that an air link was vital. They seemed to like the idea, and after several months, Roger and his friends flew over to observe progress. About 100 yards of the jungle floor had been cleared and they dropped some lengths of cloth to encourage the Atshuaras. Another reconnaissance a few months later showed the work not much advanced and it was obvious that they needed help on the ground.

Roger went himself, guided by Jivaros over the trail from Wambimi. He took a hand-crank radio, a few provisions, and a machete. It was to prove a demanding ten days' assignment. After five days Nate flew Frank Drown over the terrain to look for him because they had had no word. When they finally spotted him they reeled out some 1500 feet of telephone cable and over this ground-to-air line learned what had happened.

Roger found the Atshuaras had caught influenza from a group of soldiers who had passed through their terrain. They had no resistance to 'flu and were terrified of it. The Jivaro porters who had promised to carry in the radio turned tail, and this accounted for him not having a radio. He had to work on the airstrip alone and at one point he was surprised by a bushmaster, which he decapitated with his machete. He needed medicines urgently and asked for a landing in four days.

When the Friday came Nate cancelled the flight for twenty-four hours; as they say in Spanish, 'the day had woken up raining'. He was not taking chances. 'It isn't a Sunday school picnic,' said Nate, 'it's a serious business. You have to do your best calculating and double-checking on everything – and then, trusting the Lord, go in and do your duty.'

The next day Nate found the clearing with great difficulty. His heart sank because it was not what you would describe as an airstrip at all. It appeared impossible and he was just about to cut the engine and yell to Roj, 'Sorry, it's no soap!' when he decided to have another look. Roger had delineated the strip with bandages and drawn a line with the word 'wheels' on it. Down at the far end he had marked off 250 yards.

Nate decided to try one approach and dropped steeply at about 100 m.p.h. When he got down low there was one tree sticking out along the edge of the strip. He said to himself, 'Roj, man, this thing does have wings sticking out!' He pulled out and thought the problem over and then decided to 'let the seat of his pants guide him' and land. 'I slipped that plane as steep as she'd slip at forty-five miles an hour; I straightened out just over the fifty yard rough stretch, and plunked the wheels down just beyond the *wheels* sign and got stopped in a little over half of the 250 yards that were available.'

Nate found Roger unkempt and unshaven and behaving frenetically. He noted in his diary. 'There wasn't any "Hell, I'm glad to see you" or "Dr. Livingstone, I presume" stuff. He shouted, "Have you got any medicines?" and I tossed him the sack. He was at the bundle tooth and nail. Then he started shouting at the top of his lungs to the Indians down the strip. I'd never seen Roj quite like that. I knew that he can snap at people when things are tight but I didn't quite know what to make of this, so I grabbed him kind of firmly by the arm and said, "Slow down now, Roj; slow down; we've got time." He said, "We haven't got time; we haven't got time," so I didn't argue. He handed me two bottles of penicillin and said, "Here, shake these," so I did. He was barking orders at the Indians and I thought to myself, "My goodness, how on earth can these people think he's a friend when he talks to them like that." '

It became evident that everyone and his brother were getting shots. Everybody was sick. Santiaku was sitting painted up "fit to kill" and doing his best to look like a chief. One of the chiefs had died the week before. Roj had shot all the worst cases and they recovered, and this was the next batch of light cases that were getting worse. Everyone obeyed his orders. He was the chief in that outfit, the real master of the situation – there was no question about it.'

On the flight back to Wambini, Roger told Nate how he had prayed for the plane to be delayed for twenty-four hours because of negligible progress on the airstrip. The next day he prayed for its safe arrival. Finally he heard it late afternoon, only for its engine noise to fade as the plane seemed to turn away. He gathered the Indians together for prayer and gospel teaching and they had just begun when someone yelled that the plane was returning. Soon they saw it.

Roger spoke from the heart when he told his pilot, 'Man, you can't imagine what it does to a guy to see this little yellow job coming in over the trees!' Then he smiled and exclaimed, 'Well, God is certainly in this thing.'

The word of God was getting to the remote tribes. The Aucas lived just over the ridge in the distance.

*

The Aucas, at a wild guess of the Quichuas, who did not believe in getting too close, numbered between five hundred and a thousand. They were scattered in a thick jungle of some twelve thousand square miles, stretching to the Peruvian border about 150 miles east of Quito, the capital city bounded by three rivers.

The region's recorded history dates back to the Spanish conquest. In 1541 Gonzalo Pizarro, brother of Francisco Pizarro, who brought the Inca Empire to an end, lost hundreds of soldiers in explorations of the region. Many were murdered by hostile Indians some of whom were the ancestors of the Aucas. Many of the Jesuit missionaries of the seventeenth century were also killed by the Indians. There was a lull then with no attempts at either exploration or exploitation until the middle of the nineteenth century when rubber hunters plundered the Amazonian basin. After heaping gifts upon the natives they pillaged the villages, murdering and looting and taking young men as slaves.

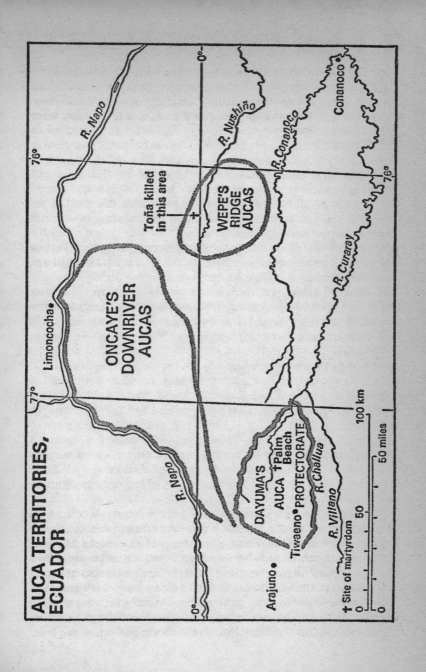

AUCA TERRITORIES, ECUADOR

R. Napo

R. Nushiño

0°

76°

76°

R. Conanoco

Conanoco

Toña killed in this area

WEPE'S RIDGE AUCAS

Limoncocha

ONCAYE'S DOWNRIVER AUCAS

R. Napo

R. Curaray

77°

100 km

Arajuno

DAYUMA'S AUCA †Palm Beach

Tiwaeno● PROTECTORATE

R. Challua

R. Villano

50 miles

0°

† Site of martyrdom

50

50

0

0

It could well be argued that it was the predatory rubber hunters who sowed the Aucas' mistrust and hatred of the stranger and shut off the region to colonization. Certainly, a legacy of hate and passion for revenge was passed down from father to son among the Indians.

The Shell Oil Company prospecting in the Oriente from 1940 to 1949 met with attacks from the Aucas and eleven of their workers were speared to death. The company tried to win their goodwill. At first they left presents at an Auca house, which was empty when they called. Next they dropped gifts from the sky but the powerful transport plane roaring low over the villages was not well calculated to make friends.

The Company's hopes of fraternizing were forfeited and no one made any further serious efforts to reach the Aucas until the young Americans who had gathered in Ecuador decided to make their crusade. These men, from the eastern United States, the West Coast, and the Midwestern states, were different in character, temperament and background; but they had spoken with one voice when Christ said, 'Go ye.' Their answer came in perfect unison, 'Here am I.'

Although they were prepared to die for Christ, they were careful not to jeopardize their lives unnecessarily. First they aimed to marshal every known fact about the Aucas. They read the reports of Shell Oil. They talked to anyone who had had any contact with the tribe.

Señor Carlos Sevilla, an Ecuadorian who owned a hacienda (plantation) in the region, lived in Auca country for twenty-six years before he was driven out by repeated attacks, and his body still bore scars inflicted by Aucas. He probably knew more about them than anyone.

He told the Americans that Auca boys were trained from an early age to use their nine-foot hardwood lances with deadly accuracy. He remembered finding in a deserted Auca hut a life-sized human figure carved of balsa wood with the face and heart drawn in red achiote (the red colouring from the seeds of a native plant). The wooden dummy was riddled with lance marks. He had been able to observe the fighting tactics of the Aucas which encouraged surprise. They would wait in ambush at the bend of a river where the current forces a canoe close to the shore, and while the boatmen poled back into the mainstream, they hurled their spears, yelling all the while to add to the confusion. Sevilla advised any travellers in Auca terrain to take at least two canoes so that one could fire to protect the other if surprised.

Why do the Aucas kill? The Americans asked Dayuma, an Auca woman refugee working on Señor Sevilla's plantation. Some years before Dayuma had survived a tribal killing in which her parents and some of her brothers and sisters died during an attack by a neighbouring group. It was the result of a typical family feud with its appalling chain reaction of murders. Dayuma told the young missionaries much about how the Aucas lived. Small in stature (five feet and a few inches), their skin the colour of tea and their hair straight and black, they went naked except for the vines they tied tightly around waists, wrists and ankles. In each long Auca house with its mud-packed floors and hammocks slung from the roofs for beds, there might live twenty to fifty members of a clan. The women worked in the plantations of manioc and cotton. Each man in the household had his collection of nine or ten spears which he took when out hunting or with a raiding party. The Aucas could identify individual footprints as white men recognize faces. They were fond of children and pets, and, like all jungle dwellers, were afraid of evil spirits.

Dayuma repeatedly told the Americans, 'Never, never trust them. They may appear friendly and then they will turn round and kill.'

The men realized that the best way to convince the Aucas that these white men were friendly and well-intentioned would be to talk to them in their own language. Dayuma must be God's answer to their language difficulties. Jim Elliot got down to compiling their own Auca phrase book by talking to Dayuma and listening intently. He wrote in an exercise book such phrases as *Biti miti punimupa* (I like you, I want to be your friend), *Biti winki pungi amupa* (Let's get together). And *Awum irimi?* (What is your name?). He rehearsed his pronunciation with Dayuma and so built a simple vocabulary which they all hoped would be recognizable to the Aucas.

Meanwhile, Nate Saint carried out aerial surveys to find the Indians. On the first 'recce' Auca clearings were spotted some fifty miles east of Arajuno, the abandoned Shell Oil base where Ed and

Marilou McCully worked. On a second trip Auca houses were identified only fifteen minutes' flying time from Arajuno. After so much fruitless searching a year or two previously, their immediate success now was seen as providential. It was the Lord's time to do something about the Aucas.

Ed McCully and his wife provided the vanguard at Arajuno. Their fellow missionaries, Jim and Elisabeth Elliot, were in Shandia; Peter and Olive Fleming in Payupungu; and Nate Saint, with his light plane and Marj at the radio, remained at Shell Mera, their permanent base at the hub of the outlying jungle stations. Roger Youderian and his family had returned from their outpost at Wambini and were again helping Frank and Marie Drown at Macuma, the jungle station among the Jivaros, and at this stage had not been involved in Operation Auca.

A regular programme of gift-drops was next planned using the spiralling line technique that Nate Saint and Roger Youderian had used in Atshuara country. They dropped kettles, rock salt, machetes, shirts and shorts, beads, buttons and trinkets, all with brightly coloured ribbons flying like kites behind them.

The men had not expected to see the Aucas for some weeks but on the second gift drop they were there, running after the treasures thrown from the sky and enjoying this new sport. The men flew in lower and shouted their Auca phrases until their voices became hoarse. They also tied an Indian basket on the end of the line in the hope that the Aucas might be inspired to reciprocate in an exchange of gifts. For the fourth flight Nate rigged up a battery-powered loudhailer and as they approached the clearing Jim Elliot called out his well-rehearsed Auca greetings. During the sixth week of their visits the Aucas tied their first offering on the line. It was a *llaitu*, a headband of woven feathers, and the men were elated.

At the end of the eighth flight Nate Saint, who had decided to keep a log of the whole exercise, wrote, 'One of the problems we face now is getting another man to bring our manpower up to strength.' He thought of Roger Youderian. The others scarcely knew him because he worked with different Indians in another part of the Oriente, but Nate and Roger had worked together to open up the Atshuara country and build a couple of other outstation airstrips. Nate recognized the ex-paratrooper as 'a disciplined man who was capable of great effort'. All the qualities that made Roger a good soldier he had consecrated to his new captain. Nate wrote of him, 'He knows the importance of unswerving conformity to the will of his captain. Obedience is not a momentary option; it is a diecast decision made beforehand.' Nate decided to ask Roger to join the party. He knew the others would back his judgment

*

At this time Roger Youderian was enmeshed in an inner conflict of the soul which he had yet to resolve. Only his wife, Barbara, knew of his deep spiritual searchings, his longing for revelation. Was he accomplishing *anything at all* in the mission field? He had broken through the language barrier but where were the results? He tortured himself with his evident lack of any success. Whose lives had been transformed? How many had abandoned heathen customs?

He wrote in his diary,

The cause of Christ in the Jivaria will not suffer for our having been there, but I must be honest and confess that it has not been *helped*. Seems to me there is no future in the Jivaria for us, and the wisest thing for us to do will be to pull stakes ... I do not put any blame on personalities or circumstances involved; the failure is mine. It didn't pan out. It is not because of wife and family. Macuma station is ample for a home for them and all we need has been offered ...

The issue is personal. Have been battling and thinking the issue for many months. It is a combination of situations and talents that has me buffaloed. This is the first time in my life that I have turned my back ... I'm afraid that anything along missionary lines has been scared out of me. If I couldn't make the grade here in Mocuma I'm not foolish enough to expect a change of setting would change *me*.

Roger had come out from Mocuma to help build a mission-sponsored hospital at Shell Mera, the home of the Saint family. 'We might pass Christmas here, finish the hospital in Shell, and head home,' he wrote. The reason was his failure to measure up as a missionary.

'It seems strange,' he recorded, 'to try and view it in an impersonal way. Of this much I'm sure: it will draw me to read His word more, be more tolerant of others and less venturesome in my activities.'

Soon after he had written these humbling words, Roger was nailing down sheets of aluminium on the roof of the hospital when Nate Saint sought him out. Nate told him about the plan to put down the light plane on a sandbar in the heart of Auca country, build a shelter and wait to make contact. It promised to be the biggest adventure for all of them. Nate said simply, 'We are short of a man. Will you go, Roj?'

Roger agreed at once, but he had secret reservations. *He* wanted to go, but did God want him to? He could not go just out of a spirit of adventure, as another man might sail the Atlantic or scale a mountain. He must have God's bidding, and there had been no message from his Lord. He agonized to find out, and eventually triumphed. His wife said later, 'He went with a happy expectant mind and his heart full of joy.'

Roger wrote in his diary, 'I will die to self. I will begin to ask God to put me in a service of constant circumstances where to live Christ I must die to self.'

*

Now that they had the team together their preparations gathered speed. Tinted photographs of the five men, holding the feathered headdresses and combs which the Aucas had sent them, were dropped to familiarize the Indians with their faces. Each portrait carried the hallmark of the operation, a drawing of a little yellow airplane. They selected their landing-place which they called 'Palm Beach', and kept up weekly friendship flights over 'Terminal City', the name the men gave to the Auca village.

It was decided to land the team on 'Palm Beach' with a pre-fabricated tree-house and aluminium for a roof. They planned to install a model plane on the site to help identify themselves. Their neighbours would then be invited to call, the Piper making a circuit of the immediate area every hour or so, the men shouting their well-learned phrases to coax them. Each of them worked to memorize the phrase book. They would probably allow themselves five days to contact the Indians. If unsuccessful, they would withdraw either by air or possibly by a raft of air mattresses and bamboo. Supplies in the tree-house would be adequate for two weeks should they be cut off by flood or siege.

Roger drew up a master-plan, allotting each member of the

team his role. Jim prefabricated the house to be put up in a tree to ensure safety at night. He also took charge of the arms and ammunition. (It was decided that hidden arms would be carried; if the situation became fraught then the arms would be shown; if this were not enough, shots would be fired with the intention only to frighten.) Ed amassed goods for trading with the Aucas. Nate's tasks were communications and transport. Pete would help Nate with the flights and be responsible for supplies on the beach. Roger himself devised code-signs to be drawn in the sand on Palm Beach in emergency and drew maps for each missionary showing tactical landmarks. He also prepared the first-aid box.

Marj would man the radio in Shell Mera and Barbara would stay in Arajuno, helping Marilou prepare the men's food which Nate would fly daily to Palm Beach.

In a month the rains would make landings impossible and everything now pointed to an early start. The gift-drops had been more and more encouraging and the last bark-cloth bundle from the Aucas had been 'by far the most all-out effort at a fair-trade arrangement'. They took the heavy gift off the line and found it comprised cooked fish, peanuts, cooked manioc, cooked plantain, two squirrels, one parrot (with bananas), pottery, a piece of cooked meat and a smoked monkey tail. The young men were delighted. They sampled the goodies – and then sat down and ate the meal that Marilou had prepared!

Tuesday, January 3, 1956, the date fixed for the first landing in Auca territory, was a beautiful day and their spirits rose with the sun. Roger and Nate checked the plane and found fluid had leaked from the right brake. At 7 a.m. they radioed Marj asking for brake fluid to be flown them at once by M.A.F. pilot, Johnny Keenan. The technical hitch gave them time for a leisurely breakfast and prayers together.

Ed and Nate took off just after 8.00 a.m. and realized when they saw fog over the river Curaray that they would not have made it any earlier. They landed at Palm Beach and the men jumped out much relieved to have averted mishap, for if they had set down the light plane on softer sand it would have nosed over. They found hard sand for the take-off and with difficulty Nate made it into the air. Back at Arajuno the scheduled list for the next flight was scrapped. Instead of supplies, Nate flew in Roger and Jim with essentials like the walkie-talkie and more food. Next time he delivered a radio, tools and boards for the tree-house. Personal items, a larger radio, more food, and the last boards and aluminium for roofing were carried on flights four and five.

The men on the beach built the tree-house 35 foot off the ground and found they had made their task more difficult by choosing an ironwood tree (chonta palm), a wood which lives up to its name. Nate flew over 'Terminal City' before heading back to Arajuno and addressed the Aucas over the loud hailer, 'Come tomorrow to the Curaray Ada (river)!' The Indians seemed bewildered by the invitation.

Wednesday, January 4. Jim wrote to Elisabeth, 'We saw puma (jungle lion) tracks on the open sand and heard them last night. It is a beautiful jungle, open and full of palms. Our hopes are up but no sign of the neighbours yet.'

Ed wrote to Marilou, 'Meals are fine and plentiful. I'll send some dirty clothes back with Nate. Bugs are bad. I love you very much. Thanks for everything.'

Thursday, January 5. Nate noted in his log, 'All quiet at Palm Beach. However we feel sure we are being watched. One bend below camp, we sighted unmistakable footprints . . . Except for forty-seven billion flying insects the place is a little paradise. With the help of smoke and repellant we are all enjoying the experience immensely . . .

'Ever since Pete and I landed and reported the human footprints among the tapir, puma, alligators, we were objects of boisterous ridicule from the other fellows. Jim and Roj decided to check at close range, wading and running along the beaches. "Aucas, at least thirty of them," they confirmed, "but the prints are maybe a week old." '

Nate finished this entry, 'We find we have a friendlier feeling for the Aucas all the time. We must not let that lead us to carelessness. It is no small thing to try to bridge the twentieth century and the Stone Age – God help us take care.'

Friday, January 6. At 11.00 a.m. the men were all on Palm Beach shouting in warm Midwestern accents their Auca phrases to the secretive jungle. Suddenly a man's strong voice answered them from across the Curaray. Three Aucas stepped into sight; a young man, a woman of about thirty, and a teen-age girl. Silenced momentarily, the Americans then shouted as one man *'Puinanil!'* (Welcome!)

They could not understand the voluble reply of the Auca man, but his sign language was unmistakable. He was offering the girl for barter or as a present. Jim waded across the river, took their hands and led them back to the sand-bar. With many smiles and polite expressions in the Auca language, the Americans managed to dispel their visitors' nervousness. Roger gave them some paring knives and Nate presented them with a model airplane and a machete. They were captivated by the camera and the missionaries took dozens of photographs. The man, whom they named 'George', appeared at ease, friendly and talkative. He made plain his eagerness to fly over his own village. So the Piper circled Terminal City with George leaning out, gesticulating and shouting gleefully to his friends.

The news of their first contact was radioed to Marj and then the men discussed tactics. They would visit the village if they could get an escort from the Aucas. An airstrip in their valley would be the next objective and by drawing in the sand they tried to demonstrate to 'George' how an airstrip might be cleared in his village. The three Aucas stayed on the beach that night.

Saturday, January 7. The Aucas had gone. The Americans expected more to arrive, perhaps to invite them to their village. No one came. Nate and Pete made three flights in the afternoon over Terminal City and were dismayed to detect some apprehension. Women and children ran to hide on their first appearance. On the second and third flights they seemed reassured and Nate logged, 'We got some good smiles from "George" and another young man who probably aspires to ride in the plane.'

Sunday, January 8. As Nate and Pete boarded the Piper at base they called, 'So long, girls. Pray. We believe today's the day.'

At Palm Beach the men enjoyed the ice-cream and freshly-baked blueberry muffins Marilou had sent them. They agreed on another reconniassance and Nate flew alone this time. He espied 'a commission of ten' making for Palm Beach. At last, they were on their way to the Curaray and when he touched down he yelled, 'This is it, guys!'

At noon, Marj in Shell Mera was radioed, 'Looks like they'll be

here for the early afternoon service. Pray for us. This *is* the day!
Will contact you next 4.30 p.m.'

*

Barbara Youderian and her family looked forward to seeing Roger
for the first time since Operation Auca got under way. He was to
fly back with Nate and come to Arajuno that night while Pete
took a turn sleeping in the tree house on Palm Beach.

All the wives were now worried by the silence. There had been
no radio contact at 4.30 p.m. as arranged; it was the only time
since Nate became a jungle pilot in 1948 that he and Marj had
been out of contact even for an hour.

The evening wore on, minutes like hours, and the women told
each other the men's radio could not be working; it had failed
them before. They clasped the explanation tightly like a talisman
and paced the airstrip straining to hear the familiar hum of the
little plane. None of the wives slept that night. Their prayers be-
sought God to keep their husbands safe.

*

Monday, January 9. M.A.F. pilot Johnny Keenan flew over Palm
Beach in Piper II, a twin to Nate's plane. At 9.30 a.m. he reported
grimly, 'No sign of the men. The Piper is on the beach stripped of
all its fabric.'

Barbara and Marilou were flown from Arajuno to Shell Mera,
the centre of the action. Before they left they put a note on the
door stating where to find food and medicines because they felt
sure there would be survivors among their husbands. But even
before they reached the big house at Shell Mera, where the wives
and their children were gathering, Marilou, the trained nurse
among them, decided it had been premature to leave the post. She
must be there to help should one or more of the men return
wounded and exhausted. Later the same day she was flown back
to Arajuno where she kept brave vigil for another three days.

On Monday evening it was agreed to organize a ground search
party led by Frank Drown, Roger's senior colleague at Macuma,
and a man with twelve years' experience among the Jivaros.

Tuesday, January 10. Betty Elliot was flown to Shell Mera from
Shandia with Nate's sister, Rachel, who had been keeping her

company there. Frank Drown was brought out from Macuma, and many of the missionaries arrived from Quito, some as volunteers for the ground party.

A radio message was received that a helicopter and airplanes were on the way from Panama.

An Ecuadorian airline pilot came to the house that night to report that he had flown over the Curaray and spotted 'a large fire without any smoke'. This suggested a gasoline fire or a signal flare which Nate always carried in his pack. Hopes flickered.

Wednesday, January 11. Marj, who had scarcely left the radio transmitter since Sunday afternoon, called the wives in a voice too tightly controlled. Johnny Keenan making his fourth flight over Palm Beach had seen a body floating face down a quarter of a mile downriver from the Piper. Some of the land party went to Arajuno to prepare the airstrip for the big planes of the United States Air Force soon to arrive from Panama.

During the day the remaining volunteers were transported to Arajuno, the base from which the rescue party would set out. Here they joined missionaries, Indians, and thirteen Ecuadorian soldiers who had already volunteered.

Although under great personal stress (she was also eight months pregnant) Marilou calmly carried on and prepared a meal for all of them before they set off. As the party left she said, matter-of-fact, to a fellow missionary, 'There is no hope. All the men are dead.'

From the air Johnny Keenan reported, 'Another body sighted – 200 feet below Palm Beach.'

The ground party pitched camp for the night at the meeting of the Oglan and the Curaray rivers. The men slept on beds of banana leaves, taking turns to keep watch.

Thursday, January 12. Before setting off the missionaries prayed. The soldiers, of a different faith, prayed with them.

At 10.00 a.m. they contacted Johnny Keenan in Piper II by a two-way radio which Air Rescue Service had supplied. He cautioned them to expect two canoes of Quichuas on the river. They were a group from Ed McCully's mission station at Arajuno who had pressed on boldly to Palm Beach in the van of anyone else. They reported seeing Ed's body at the water's edge. One of them had brought back his watch.

In the afternoon the search intensified with the helicopter and other aircraft stacked up over the jungle. Johnny flew lowest in the Piper, above him the U.S. Navy R-4D, and higher again, the large amphibian of the Air Rescue Service. A plane of the Ecuadorian Air Force encircled all of them ready to help.

The Army helicopter landed on Palm Beach and Air Force Major Nurnberg jumped on to the sand. 'No one here,' he radioed, and the helicopter took off again. It crossed to the other side, hovered over a spot 200 yards further on, making third and fourth ominous stops only 10 feet above the muddy water. Then the aircraft returned to Arajuno. Four bodies had been seen in the river bed.

Later in the afternoon Marilou was flown to Shell Mera to join the other wives and that night the military men described what they had seen. There was no hysteria, no open display of grief. Barbara Youderian wrote in her diary: 'Tonight the Major told us of his finding four bodies in the river. One had tee-shirt and blue jeans. Roj was the only one who wore them ... God gave me this verse two days ago, Psalm 48: 14, "For this God is our God for ever and ever: he shall be our guide even unto death." As I came face to face with the news of Roj's death, my heart was filled with praise. He was worthy of his homegoing. Help me, Lord, to be both mother and father, to know wisdom and instruction ... I wrote a letter to the mission family, trying to explain the peace I have.'

Friday, January 13. The ground party, who had heard the grim news over the radio, left at 6 a.m. to meet the helicopter at Palm Beach at 10. They were on edge from the tensions of the trip and the job that awaited them.

Quichuas were sent ahead when the beach was reached as they would most readily identify any traces of recent Auca visits. There were no signs. The soldiers spread out to give cover while two Indians dug a common grave below the tree-house. Others searched for the men's possessions and looked for clues. Some of the men dismantled the Piper, but it was not until the Army helicopter arrived at noon and hovered over the bodies that the search party found them.

Four bodies were recovered and the search party laid them face down in a row on the beach. They never did get the fifth,

Andrew Kaguru

Helmuth James von Moltke

Janani Luwum

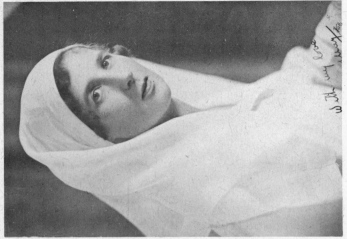

May Hayman

Vivian Redlich

Toña

Roger Youderian. This picture was taken by his colleague Nate Saint, and dropped to Auca Indians to familiarize them with the men and the missionary plane

Daw Pwa Sein

Martinez Quintana

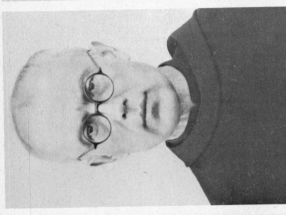

Blessed Maximilian Kolbe

Ivan ('Vanya') Vasilievich Moiseyev

which was Ed's body, the one identified by Quichuas the day before. They had brought back Ed's watch and they had also taken off one of his shoes – a tremendous size, 13½ – and thrown it on the beach. Nurnberg had picked it up and brought it back to Shell Mera, but Ed's body had gone, probably swept away by the rain and higher water in the night. Identification of the other bodies was confirmed from personal possessions like rings and watches, now assuming a pathos of their own. As Ed McCully was not one of the men so it became certain that all five young missionaries were dead.

The horror of the scene was heightened by the wrath of a tropical storm which broke around them. The Indian guides were terror-stricken because they believed that the all-powerful Auca witch doctor summoned a storm whenever his fellow tribesmen planned a spearing raid. The pallbearers improvised stretchers from the aluminium sheets which had roofed the tree-house.

Lashed by driving rain the men laboured up a muddy bank to the dug grave. A brief service was led by Frank Drown. On the way back after two hours canoeing and trekking the party pitched camp. They contrived shelters from the all-purpose metal sheets with palms for walls and floor. One missionary cooked a meal. Another, Don Johnson, offered thanks to the Lord for helping them to reach and bury their friends. He spoke with an eloquent directness about the characters of the men but he was not so much mourning the dead as affirming faith in God's will.

Dawn was slow to break and the atmosphere grew tenser. This was the hour the Aucas favoured for attack. The persistent sounds of a 'puma' alarmed the guides for they knew how realistically the Aucas could imitate the jungle lion. The burly Major, grey-faced and sharp-eyed, silenced the 'puma' with a crackle of fire from his carbine.

Saturday, January 14. The Army helicopter flew the five widows over Palm Beach to see from the air the grave shared by four of their husbands. Marj Saint said simply, 'That must be the most beautiful little cemetery in the world.'

The women lost no time in making plans to continue the men's labours. Johnny Keenan resumed the gift drops so that the Aucas would know they remained friendly without thought of reprisals.

Barbara Youderian returned with her two children to work

among the Jivaros and the others either resumed the duties of the outstations or took up new posts.

Letters streamed in to the young widows and the world's prayers petitioned God for the women and their children. The extraordinary strength of the widows helped the children to see the deaths of their fathers not as a tragedy but as something God had planned. The consequences were already reverberating around the globe. An Air Force Major stationed in England determined to join the M.A.F. A missionary in Africa who knew the men, wrote, 'Our work will never be the same. Their lives have left their mark on ours.' An American boy of eighteen in Iowa resolved 'to try to take the place of one of the five'.

The Christians among the Quichuas carried on the work started by the missionaries. In their prayer-meetings these Indians asked God to bless their enemies and 'to send more messengers to the Aucas'. Thousands prayed that Christ *would* be named among the Aucas, a people in a remote jungle territory who had been unknown to them before.

The prayers of the widows themselves were for the Aucas. They knew their husbands' deaths were not the end of the courageous crusade to the savage tribe but only the beginning of new conquests for Christ.

Toña

1944–1970

The film had an amateur, home movie quality, but at every show-ing the audience gave it rapt attention. The pictures had been taken by the men of Palm Beach and were a record of events from the landings until just before they were killed. One of those who saw the film was Dayuma who knew the men well, for she had helped them to learn their Auca vocabulary, and she had another special interest in the film. It contained pictures of some members of her family and of places she remembered well, like the sand-bar by the river where she had fished and played as a child. As she watched she decided to change her life, to return home.

She had fled from her tribe because she feared she might be the next victim of a vendetta murder and for eight years had worked on a hacienda in the Andean foothills, adopting the speech and dress of a Quicha Indian. There she met Rachel Saint, of Wycliffe Bible Translators, and sister of Nate Saint, one of the five martyred Americans. Rachel Saint taught Dayuma the best-known stories from the Bible and two years after the martyrdoms Dayuma went home to her own people as a missionary herself.

When the Aucas met her they were amazed that she was still alive and that she had not been eaten by the foreigners. Dayuma, questioning about what had happened at Palm Beach, learned that the Aucas had killed the Americans in the belief that they were cannibals. The missionaries had carried guns to protect themselves but had fired their shots into the air.

A month after Dayuma's return, Rachel Saint, and Elisabeth Elliot, together with her small daughter, Valerie, entered the tribe and slung their hammocks alongside the Aucas who had speared dead Rachel's brother and Elisabeth's husband, Valerie's father. Dayuma had prepared her savage relatives to receive her friends peacefully. She had a vivid style of teaching with appropriate sound effects, and her people had been captivated by the stories she told.

Rachel, who spoke their language, was given an Auca name, Nimu, meaning 'star'. Certainly she shed light, and Gikita, who was the oldest man in the Auca settlement at Tiwaeno, listened attentively.

There had been five killers at Palm Beach: Gikita, the leader; Kimo, Minkayi, Nimonga and Dyuwi. The youngest, Dyuwi, had hated all outsiders since as a young boy he had been wounded by gunfire. He and the others feared reprisals for Palm Beach and trusted no one from the outside. Yet, as Gikita and Kimo were drawn to listen to Dayuma, their fears began to fade, particularly as gifts for the tribe were still being dropped from the air.

The Aucas began to doubt if all foreigners were in fact cannibals, and to guess that some might even be trusted. Eventually, Dayuma persuaded them to make a landing field. The project took a year, with only seven men, helped by women and children, clearing the 600 ft. strip.

Pilot Don Smith, of Wycliffe's Jungle Aviation and Radio Service, landed safely after Rachel Saint decided to allow him to fly in – she still had horrific memories of the fate of her brother and his friends and the vandalized light plane. She thought that her teaching and Dayuma's example had influenced their ways, but she was well aware that no man from outside had ever left Auca territory unharmed.

The air service helped in important ways. In May 1961, two of the former killers and their wives flew with Rachel and Dayuma to Wycliffe's jungle base at Limoncocha, on the Napo River, to help formalize the Auca language. Agreement on the Auca alphabet (Auca was an oral language which had never been committed to paper) was a milestone, and when Rachel undertook to translate the Gospel of Mark, that was another step forward.

In August 1962, Dayuma married Koki, the son of Gikita, the former leader of the Palm Beach killers, and Rachel Saint gave the wedding feast. A year later, when complications occurred during her pregnancy, Dayuma was flown to the missionary hospital at Shell Mera and the baby became the first Auca birth to be officially registered in Ecuador. She was named Nancy and also given an Auca name meaning 'humming bird'.

In 1963, Betty Elliot and her daughter returned to the U.S.A., and Catherine Peeke, a Wycliffe partner, joined Rachel in Tiwaeno. She was working towards her Ph.D. in linguistics at Indiana University and now Auca grammar became the subject of her thesis.

Another of the Palm Beach killers, Kimo, led the growing Auca church, and under his thatched roof Aucas met for prayers and to read the Gospel of Mark as Rachel translated it. Above all, Kimo was concerned to encourage the young men of the tribe, its future leaders, to turn to Christianity.

One Sunday morning, one of their group, Toña, who would lean on the bamboo fence around Kimo's house and pretend not to listen, was prompted to declare his interest. He wanted a new start and he suspected the words from 'God's Carving' – Dayuma's term for the Bible – were more dependable than those of the ancestors. Under Kimo's tutelage Toña learnt the lessons of Christianity, and Rachel, observing his innate intelligence, coached him to read, write, and teach.

When Kimo's own home became too crowded for the Christian Aucas to meet there, a large thatched church was built as 'God's speaking house'. It was high off the ground to keep out the geese and goats which roamed the Tiwaeno clearing, and worshippers shinned up and down a notched pole to get in and out. As their new faith deepened, so did the concern of the Aucas for their warrior relatives down river. They would not be content until all the tribe was reached, and there still remained one main pagan settlement on what was known as 'the Ridge'. The ferocity of the Ridge Aucas, who numbered some two hundred, was legendary, and they lived directly in the path of oil exploration teams which pressed in upon them from both north and south.

*

One Sunday morning in November 1963, Dyuwi, the youngest of the spearing party on the Curaray River, made an announcement in God's speaking house. 'Last night I dreamed that God told me to go to the down-river people,' he said simply. The startled Christian Aucas discussed the dangers – the snake-infested trails, and likelihood of being speared. Then Rachel suggested that they should pray for someone to come out from the down-river group to open up the way, just as Dayuma had fled to the outside and returned to be the contact between tribe and missionaries.

The next spring Rachel and Catherine flew to Quito, the capital of Ecuador, and while they were there a radio message reached Rachel. It came from Limoncocha and reported that a wounded Auca girl had been found on the Napo River and was now seriously ill in a remote jungle settlement. Rachel flew to join her. Large balsa wood earplugs and coarse hair cut squarely back over her ears with a clam shell identified the girl as one of the down-river Aucas.

Her name was Oncaye and she was fleeing from spearings among her own people when she had been shot at by foreigners. The girl could be the key to the down-river problem. 'We must wait and pray,' said Rachel.

By February 1965, a small band of Auca missionaries were ready to journey down river. Dyuwi wanted to go, for he claimed that God had spoken directly to him. Toña volunteered to accompany him despite objections from his mother, and two women joined them, Oncaye and her half-sister, Boika. The party would have to travel through a hundred miles of jungle; but on the evening of the third day they were back. They had lost their bearings and described a circle. A second attempt made later ended when they returned after six days. This exploration was badly timed. The rains had come and every trail was blocked, the rivers in such flood as to be impassable.

A third expedition set out in February 1966 with Toña trained to use a portable two-way radio for contact with Tiwaeno and Limoncocha. This time ten days passed before they limped home with swollen feet, having thrown off some angry Ridge men who pursued them. At one time during the dash to escape they prayed for rain to eradicate their footprints on the beach. It came in torrents.

Pilot Don Smith decided there must be air-to-ground contact with any future party and a loudspeaker was mounted on the wing of the plane; but two more expeditions were fruitless, and all the time news of spearings reached them. Another incentive for sustaining the attempts was the arrival down river of petroleum exploration teams from the Colombian border.

Don Smith managed to drop a transmitter by parachute. It was encased in a container made of bits and pieces – a lard can, a tuna fish tin, a flashlight – and worked flawlessly, but the Aucas persisted in ripping off the antenna which was arranged around a plastic salad bowl. Don Smith decided to hide the transmitter inside an Indian basket. The antenna was woven into the basket and the transmitter hidden under a false bottom with gifts placed on top. The result was all that he wished.

This was the beginning of contact with Oncaye's extended family and many more of the ferocious tribe. In February 1968, they started coming to the Tiwaeno community. Ten years before there had been fifty-six Aucas on the clearing. Now there were 104 and more than double the social problems. The new arrivals lied and stole and revived old family grievances; and the Auca Christians had their work cut out to quench the viciousness among the newcomers and to win a change of heart among so many. There was a cultural collision between the up-river and down-river groups and it was made worse by epidemics of 'flu and 'foreign' illness.

Yet the Auca Christians prevailed and made converts.

*

Early in 1969, during several important flights, some of the groups on the Ridge were identified. From the lowered transmitter came one broadcast in which through the static came the words, 'Toña, who's calling?' It was an Auca name. The Toña of Tiwaeno now seemed to have a namesake on the Ridge. The name could be pivotal for future contacts. At the time both Tiwaeno Toña and his wife, Wato, were down the Tiwaeno River planting peanuts, and not until the end of January was it possible for him and his mother, Mini, with Catherine Peeke of Wycliffe, to be flown over the location of the broadcast.

Toña took the microphone and spoke with authority.

'I, Toña, come . . . I, the one who was born the son of Mini, I come. I, born the son of Coba, I come. Wave if you recognize me!' Many arms waved vigorously, and Toña singled out his elder brother, Wepe, and his uncle, Caiga. He called commandingly, 'Don't spear the outsiders. Let them alone.'

There was rejoicing in Tiwaeno when Toña and his mother reported finding relatives on the Ridge. Toña was now designated link-man for contacting the Ridge Aucas. Other reconnaissances followed when Toña called over the loudspeaker to introduce himself and to ask the Aucas below to identify themselves.

Then, just as the promise of successful ground contact seemed almost assured, the flights had to stop. The situation at Tiwaeno, where the Aucas were now overcrowded and short of food, was pushed to the edge of disaster during the summer by an outbreak of polio, and flights over the rugged north Ridge were suspended for fear of carrying the disease to the Aucas there.

In November, when flying over the Ridge started again, Toña spoke from the plane to almost all the locations telling the listening Aucas of the months when he had given up his teaching to help the sick and the dying. Christianity was a way of reconciliation with God, he broadcast, and a message of love to end senseless vendettas and the murder of strangers. Fortunately, oil exploration teams had temporarily stopped trying to enter the Ridge country, but now the oil company helipads would soon reappear in the surrounding jungle. From the air Toña pleaded, 'Stay at home. Do not kill the men coming to look for liquid fire.'

On one flight the transmission from the radio basket on the ground included the voice of Toña's sister, Omade. Contact was made and he told her how he now longed to be the first missionary to set foot on the soil of the Ridge Aucas; but his sister insisted he wait. Too many men on the Ridge were killers, she said, and there was much fear still of outsiders and of their Magic Thing, the *caento* (airplane).

While he waited, Toña improved his reading and writing skills, and re-opened the literacy school to carry on teaching. He was a born teacher, gifted with patience and persistence, and he showed much initiative in pioneering his own teaching methods.

Early in April 1970, his sister, Omade, agreed to the Ridge operation, but made the proviso that Toña should arrive by one of the trails. He compromised and arranged to approach as close as possible by helicopter.

The action was fixed for April 27, a day which dawned in fog and rain. As he waited for the clouds to clear Toña wrote a note to Rachel – the first correspondence in the Auca language: 'Because of your sincere prayers to God, He is going to work wonderfully for me. While I was yet in Tiwaeno, God spoke to me, "You go, and when you have gone and carried them all my message, then after they have heard, whoever says 'Yes!' will believe." '

The weather cleared later in the day and the oil company helicopter arrived to pick up Toña. On the strip at Limoncocha, he practised lowering his radio by rope and jumping from the helicopter wearing his small pack. The plan involved using the helicopter, as well as the missionaries' own plane, to create a diversion. The helicopter took off first and was followed by the plane carying Rachel and Dyuwi which then flew ahead leading the way to a small clearing close to his sister's house where Toña would jump. Once over the site on the Ridge the plane veered off sharply, diving noisily to claim the attention of the Aucas while the helicopter slipped down for the drop under the cover of the trees.

Helicopter Pilot Bob Conway could get no nearer than twenty feet because the clearing was so small and a tall tree had been left standing in the middle of it. He watched the agile young Auca carefully lower his radio and jump after it. Toña scrambled to his feet and waved before darting into the forest.

Next day he reported by radio to Tiwaeno, where on the blackboard of his school classroom he had written the verse from Mark (16. 15) ... 'Go ye into all the world, and preach the gospel to every creature.' He said he had been prepared to spend the night alone in the clearing, praying for guidance, since he was unsure of the trail; but around midnight he heard men returning from a wild hog hunt. His brother's name was spoken, so he picked up his gear and followed the men to a small house, staying outside in the shadows until he was certain it was Wepe. Then he gave the Auca call to announce himself and was welcomed inside by his brother.

Every day Toña faithfully reported progress. 'Today I told them of the Creator God ... Of Jesus, His only son ... Of David, God's man who did not spear his enemies ... He told them of Tiwaeno, the community of peace where Auca relatives lived according to God's Carving. He told them of the need to live with foreigners in peace. Occasionally, he asked for a flight to bring gifts of axes, machetes and beads. Once he reported going to another clearing to give serum to a man dying from snakebite and saving the man's life.

Late in May, Toña told of a big party to be held at his brother's clearing and of his forebodings that it could end badly. The older Aucas in Tiwaeno agreed that this occasion might bring a resurgence of hatred for the stranger.

On June 5, Toña radioed, 'There is trouble ... I may have to flee in the night.' Next morning he called again, 'God has told me to stay and teach his people, and therefore I will not leave.'

Several days later Toña's mother, Mini, talked to him by radio and so did his shy young wife, Wato, and their daughter. Toña told the little girl, 'Praying very very much to our Heavenly Father, he accomplishing it, I will come home to you again.' There was no word from Toña on June 25, nor on the next day. On the third day the plane from Tiwaeno flew over burned houses. There was no sign of life and the gleaming aluminium pots sent as presents were turned upside down on top of spears.

The radio basket was parachuted to a house that was still intact and conflicting answers were given to the question tormenting them at Tiwaeno. 'Where is Toña?' 'Toña has escaped a killing raid and fled' ... 'Toña has been killed and buried.' ...

*

By mid-September, the Indians came out of hiding and began to rebuild their homes. On December 21, Catherine Peeke and Mini flew over the clearing and another basket transmitter was dropped. The recording made included a thin voice apparently coming from one of the huts and it sounded like Toña. 'I've always believed in God from my youth ... They almost killed my brother Wepe and me, but God guarded us; we fled far away and returned recently ... they destroyed my radio. Wepe is gone today, they are all out hunting hogs.'

On succeeding days when flights were made Wepe was there and he seemed to be telling Toña what to say. It sounded as if he was being held a prisoner and his good treatment depended on the Tiwaeno Christians dropping axes, machetes and other gifts.

On December 29, after much coaxing on the loudspeaker, Toña came out of the house and was clearly seen by his mother and by Catherine Peeke.

Arrangements were made to fly him out with his brother Wepe. Wepe asked that his daughter, who was at Tiwaeno, bring him machetes and axes, and then he and Toña would return together. They cleared a rough area for the helicopter to land Oncaye and her baby, her brother, and the pilot. They were well received and arranged for the pick-up, first for Toña and Wepe, and then for themselves.

Waiting anxiously among an eager crowd on the Tiwaeno strip were Toña's wife, Wato, and his mother Mini. The man who emerged did not look much like Toña. The whole thing had been a cruel deception.

*

A few days later Wepe asked to be taken back to the Ridge with his nephew Monga and after they got home they started to clear an airstrip similar to the one at Tiwaeno. They kept in constant radio contact and when their radio needed replacement Wepe's daughter, Oncaye, agreed 'to go in for a few hours, to hand over the new radio, to give a short course in behaviour towards outsiders, and to make suggestions towards airstrip construction.' Oncaye went with another Auca Christian woman and both returned safely after a friendly reception.

They learned that Toña had met a violent death two months after he reached the Ridge Aucas. His brother's son, Kiwa, had impersonated him, and his sister's sons had been the ringleaders in killing him, although they would never have done so if they had not been misled into believing he was an outsider.

Her sister, Omade, said her sons had killed Toña without her knowledge – he had been axed in the back – and her husband had acted as the decoy to get Toña out into the jungle. 'I'm not afraid, I'll just die and go to heaven,' Toña had said. 'We'll help you go then,' his killers had jeered. 'As for us, we don't want to go.' He died forgiving them.

*

Within weeks of the women's visit to the Ridge, a dying man and his family were brought by helicopter to the nearest airstrip and then on to Tiwaeno by plane. Communications were now open. Others were flown out when ill and dying, including a powerful witch-doctor, Iketai. He was nursed back to health and was so grateful that he promised to abandon threats towards outsiders.

On November 9, 1971, the Caba River Airstrip, located near the Ridge river after which it is named, was inaugurated by the Jungle Aviation and Radio Service pilot, Virgil Gottfried. Increasing numbers of Ridge kinsmen now joined the growing Auca Christian settlement at Tiwaeno. Exchange visits were initiated, and teachers prepared to help the people remaining on the Ridge.

On February 12, 1972, the Minister of Education for Ecuador, Dr. Francisco Jaramillo Dávila, unveiled a marble plaque to the martyrs. Toña's mother, his widow and two children, and Roger Youderian's widow, were the guests of honour at the ceremony in Limoncocha.

Ten years after Roger Youderian and his friends were murdered, Kimo, one of their killers, who became the first Auca pastor, was invited to the World Congress on Evangelism in Germany to represent the newest Church in Christendom.

In the Auca story the harvest of sacrifice is demonstrably abundant, the seed of the martyr becomes the blood of the new Auca Church. The Americans wanted God's message of love understood by the whole tribe so that they would live in peace and stop murdering, not only the outsiders but each other, in endless vendettas, and there were other primitive miseries they hoped Christian understanding would eradicate. Indian children were often sacrificed to propitiate evil spirits thought to have brought misfortunes. Young children were buried in the grave of a dead mother; a sick husband might also be interred alive. If a 'worthy' son died, a 'worthless' daughter might be slain to avenge his death. Such pagan acts were committed within this last decade.

Now, more than twenty years after Palm Beach, Aucas no longer want to be called Auca (meaning 'savage') but to be known as Waodani, their indigenous ancestral name which means simply, 'the People'.

The real legacy bequeathed by Youderian and Toña for the burgeoning Wao (Auca) Church remains the men's demonstration of the meaning of Christianity: the growing number of Indian Christians believe that the norm of the Christian religion is that they should die if necessary to prove their faith.

Martinez Quintana

1901–1950

There can be no degrees of martyrdom: no man can give more than his life, and while a martyr does not seek death he is obedient to whatever he believes to be the will of God. Obedience is not a momentary choice but an unshakeable decision made beforehand.

In Colombia, Martinez Quintana, a carpenter who became a pastor, was fully aware of the threat to his life when he moved to an Evangelical Chapel in the mountains. A Colombian writer, Francisco Ordonez, in a book to commemorate the first century of evangelical work in the country, writes passionately, 'Every one of these Colombian Christians may justifiably utter the words of the Jewish patriarch, "God made me fertile in the land of my affliction." '

When news that the pastor at Campo Hermoso had been murdered, and the church and parsonage burned, reached George Constance, the director of the Christian and Missionary Alliance in Colombia, he decided he must ride there. It was in 1950 during *La Violencia*, a ferocious civil war lasting ten years and costing a quarter of a million lives. Constance reasoned that some Evangelical Christians might have survived the scourge by police, army, and Roman Catholics, who vilified them as heretics, and he was needed to help the persecuted and console the mourners.

The journey was long and hazardous. It was September and the start of the second rainy season had made the temperate valleys below the snow line wet. There were no roads and the going was hard. It took him three days by mule from his home in Cali to reach the scattered congregation of Campo Hermoso, which lies seven thousand feet high in the Central Cordillera, the most magnificent of the Colombian Andes extending like a massive wall for five hundred miles. It was not a town or even a village but a vast rural area spread over the mountains like a huge green and white counterpane, with coffee plantations and cattle farms in the alpine pastures. It had become the centre of the Evangelical

CENTRAL WEST
COLOMBIA

75°

R. Cauca

R. Magdalena

R. Atrato

PACIFIC OCEAN

6°

CALDAS

CUNDIN-
AMARCA

Manizales •

Pereira •

Armenia •

Ibague •

Bogota •

QUINDIO

4°

Buenaventura •

Chaparral •

† Campo
Hermoso

Cali •

Neiva •

Central Cordillera

2°

2°

† Site of martyrdom

High land

0   50   100   150 km

0   50   100 miles

Church for an immense and faithful congregation whose commitment brought constant danger.

The places he rode through were strangely silent with the people afraid and in hiding; and perhaps voices occasionally whispered in his ear, 'This is all folly.' But the lone American knew he had his guide. 'God went with me,' said George Constance. 'The Catholic priests schemed to kill me but, like the Magi of old, the Lord directed me to take another trail and so I escaped them. On the same journey a group of armed fanatics attempted to shoot me and throw me over a cliff; but again the Lord enabled me to saddle my mule and get away into the forest.'

At last he drew near to Campo Hermoso on his refractory and sore-footed mule. So far he had twice been delivered from death on the journey and he narrowed his eyes to search the mountains which towered disdainfully above him. He still half-expected to glimpse the chapel, an eternal surprise in the middle of the craggy range, because he had learnt that in troubled and confused times 'bad news' is often fearful rumour.

On Sunday mornings the chapel had beckoned enouragement to hundreds of worshippers coming on foot and on horseback along the treacherous mountain paths from places many miles away. Now his keen eyes could not find the familiar silhouettes of building and people. The chapel had been razed to the ground. So had the parsonage and many of the wooden homes of the people. Tears welled in his eyes as he remembered the valiant story of the chapel of Campo Hermoso and all it symbolized; and the tumultuous history of Colombia where the inextricable mixture of politics and religion had led to a series of civil wars, each spectacular for extremes of cruelty unleashed upon thousands of victims. It was a record of unparalleled savagery.

*

The first President of Colombia was Simon Bolivar, the Liberator, the son of a Spanish nobleman who vowed to devote his life to the cause of freedom. He was thirty-six years of age when in 1819 he landed in Venezuela to march 2,500 soldiers over the rain-drenched Orinoco basin and across the snow-covered Andes to Nueva Granada, as the Spaniards called present-day Colombia. Bolivar defeated an army twice as large as his own and proclaimed the Republic of Gran Colombia, which embraced the states of Venezuela, Ecuador, Panama and Colombia. Ten years later all these states had broken away and formed independent republics. The rulers of Colombia could not agree and there are reputed to have been as many as seventy civil wars during the rest of the century – almost one a year.

General Hilano Lopez of the radical faction of the Liberal Party became President in 1849. Zealous to gain more liberty for the deprived majority, his government ended slavery and communal ownership of Indian lands, and diverted tax resources from central to local control. Some of the well-intentioned reforms, however, also banished safeguards against exploitation of the poor by the rich, and actually strengthened the position of wealthy landowners, merchants and professionals against the mass of Indian peasants and artisans.

The class struggle seethed, but two crucial and bitterly divisive issues remained the principal causes of violence. These were whether a centralist or federalist system of government would be best for Colombia, and what was the appropriate role for the Roman Catholic Church.

The large number of Roman Catholics were predominantly Conservative and the small number of Evangelicals mostly Liberal. The Conservatives and Liberals fought each other almost as frequently in battle as at the polls. The Conservatives wanted a centralist political system administered from the capital, Bogota; the Liberals favoured a Federation of self-governing states.

The government expropriated Church lands in 1861 and a constitution adopted two years later guaranteed freedom of religious practice, so ending the traditional and intimate relationship between Church and State. Both actions were promptly reversed by the Conservatives when they returned to power in 1880.

The influence of the Roman Catholic Church was sinister and ubiquitous. The Archbishop of Bogota was reputed to have nominated every President from 1880 to 1930, when the Conservatives were continuously in office. In a small town the priest could often wield more power than the mayor. Sometimes the priest acted as chief of police as well, and in remote areas the police were known to conscript a day's free labour for the local church from the entire male population.

The Conservatives were ousted from rule in 1930 when Olaya Herrera became Liberal President. The Liberals now ruled for sixteen years and introduced a series of reforms called 'The Revolution on the March'. Most importantly they established effective occupation as the legal basis for tenure, so upholding the rights of thousands of peasant squatters against the claims of landowners who never used the land in any productive way. But the Liberals lost power in 1946 when two of their candidates insisted upon standing for office as President. They split the vote and a Conservative, Mariano Ospina Perez, won the election. He then initiated fierce reprisals against the Liberals by dismissing them from the army, the police and the civil service.

While the Pan-American Conference was being held in Bogota in April 1948, Dr. Jorge Eliecer Gaitan, an outstanding leader of the left wing of the Liberal Party, was murdered in broad daylight in downtown Bogota. A well-known senator and Conservative, Dr. Laureano Gomez, whose name was publicly linked with the assassination, left the country for Spain because feelings ran so high.

In fact, the rioting and violence which followed in the capital, and in many other cities, led to several thousand deaths within days. This aftermath came to be known as the *bogotazo* and was the start of one of the bloodiest epochs in Latin American history, *La Violencia*. Armed mobs of police and civilians raided the villages, killing and burning houses, as well as disarming anyone not supporting the government. In 1949 Dr. Laureano Gomez returned from Spain and in August violence broke out again with renewed fury. Dr. Gomez took the presidency by a forced election and tried to impose a Fascist State. Thousands fled from rural areas to the cities where they thought they would be safer among large populations; but people were also murdered in the towns and urban homes were bombed and burned.

The persecution was both political and religious. Evangelicals were regarded both as traitors to the State 'religion', and, as a natural corollary, disloyal to the Conservative Government who were identified with the Roman Catholics.

*

First of all, after his perilous journey, George Constance sought out the wife of the murdered pastor, Martinez Quintana, to find out what had happened. Constance knew they had been married only a few months. It was, in fact, only a month since Martinez had accepted the challenge to move to the chapel in the mountains accompanied by his beautiful second wife, Ana Maria Bonilla Ruiz. At that time he was pastor and district worker in the small town of Chaparral, more than a day's travel by horseback from Campo Hermoso chapel. He had served in Chaparral for five years and built the chapel there. Not content with his ministry in town, he often rode out into the rural areas to preach, and the mounted pastor had become a familiar sight as he drove himself, and his horse, hard along the steep mountain trails.

His decision to take the pastorate at Campo Hermoso was courageous and costly. It was a drafting to the front line, for once again there was violent persecution of the Evangelical Christians in many parts of Colombia including the Central Cordillera. Campo Hermoso, because of its widely pervasive influence and acknowledged prominence in the movement, was particularly vulnerable.

Maria told George Constance that after her husband had taken morning service in the isolated chapel on Sunday, July 2, 1950, she and Martinez and several others returned to the nearby home of Luis Castro, a friend and elder of the congregation.

They knew that an armed mob of police and civilians were storming the place, pursuing the Evangelical Christians and firing their wooden houses. Behind closed doors in Castro's house, Martinez led prayers for the lives of all of them. Suddenly attackers were outside battering the doors. 'Down with the heretics!' they shouted. The pastor went out alone to face them, praying for God to give him words to calm them. He spoke with quiet courage. The Evangelical Christians were not involved in politics, he said. They were not co-operating with the 'guerrillas'. They were not 'disturbing the country' as the police alleged. 'We are on God's work in the world,' he declared. 'We are earnest Christians serving the Lord and carrying out his will.'

He spent his words, his only ammunition, with care, but they were fragile under force, like the blossom of coffee-bushes in wind. He was shot dead at point-blank range by a policeman. He was 49.

After killing the pastor and fellow Christians, the persecutors climbed up to the chapel, poured paraffin over everything (it was kept there for the lamps) and ignited the building with a stick of dynamite. The explosion and fire completely destroyed it. As the believers ran for the hills, they hid their pastor's body among the banana trees in an unmarked grave.

The next day the invaders returned to burn more homes and killed Zoilo Torres, a young preacher and son of the founder of the church at Campo Hermoso who had died eight years earlier.

When George Constance met the remaining church members they were fewer than a hundred. Some had been killed and others thrown into gaol. He tried to find out how best to help them with the money he had brought from the Mission to alleviate distress. Their homes had been burnt and a lot of their possessions destroyed. The people were living under trees, in shacks, and with the few whose houses still stood. 'When I asked how I could best distribute the money to buy blankets, household utensils, medicines and food, their reply came swiftly and simply, "Pastor Constance, we want you to keep that money to help us rebuild our chapel." The tears ran down my cheeks and I wept, thinking of the selfishness of many North American Christians when here in the high Andes were God's children destitute, without the necessities of life. They were without homes, food or shelter, but wished to put the reconstruction of their chapel before their own basic needs.'

*

Martinez Quintana was born in 1901 in Manizales, the capital of Caldas, a small but crowded Department in the Central Cordillera. He was led to Christianity by missionaries from the Gospel Missionary Union, who had their headquarters in nearby Cali, the ancient capital of the Valle Department in the fertile Cauca Valley.

Later Martinez lived in Armenia, the capital of the Quindio Department in the heart of the coffee-growing area, and here he became one of the first 'disciples' of an American clergyman, the Rev. Clyde W. Taylor. He and his wife were the first resident missionaries in this large tract of Colombia early in 1931 and they classed him as one of their best workers.

The Taylors left Colombia ten years later. Clyde became Secretary of Public Affairs of the National Association of Evangelicals in the U.S.A. before he was made General Director. He acted as Executive Secretary of the Evangelical Foreign Missions Association for the first twenty-nine years of its existence until he retired. But Dr. Taylor and his wife well remember the energetic young Colombian.

Clyde writes from his present home in Arnold, Maryland, U.S.A., 'We had not been there long before we encountered this man we were to know as Pastor Martinez. He was of average height and build, and he had dark hair, but not jet black like most Colombians. He must have been in his early thirties and he was already a thoroughgoing Evangelical.

'He was operating a cabinet shop, where they made furniture by hand opposite the post-office in Armenia, and that is where I ran into him. I went into the post-office one day to talk to them about the Gospel and discovered that this man was a Christian. From that moment we maintained close contact. Almost immediately we started services in the city of Armenia and he was always a faithful attender.'

One of his early memories of Martinez was his brush with Seventh Day Adventists who had sent two men into the city to find Evangelicals from whom to make converts for their first congregation. Clyde Taylor had alerted him to the beliefs of this cult, and it was only a day or two later that these men made a start on their campaign in Martinez' carpentry shop.

'They couldn't have made a worse mistake. Martinez had memorized large portions of the Scripture, and when they started to expound their doctrines, quoting a single verse of the Bible out of context, he would give the verses on both sides and show their arguments to be misleading. So we soon saw that this man had considerable potential for the Ministry.'

Martinez was married, although at that time his wife was not with him. She had spells of mental instability and was periodically cared for in institutions. Later they were reunited and as they had no children adopted a little girl. Unhappily, his wife suffered another mental lapse and was eventually admitted to an asylum in Bogota.

After some time she was either released or absconded and then disappeared. It was presumed after a number of years that she was dead and Martinez married again. The first time the couple had been married by the Catholic Church; this time it was an Evangelical wedding. The missionaries lived precariously in Armenia at this time. The people were receptive to the Gospel but there was considerable fanaticism. Clyde Talor recalls, 'Many of the priests were semi-ignorant and extremely bigoted. One in our city was quite immoral and very anti-Evangelical. He was the one who decided he would put a reward on my head to see if anyone might be persuaded to kill me.'

He added laconically, 'The uncomplimentary thing about it was that he was only going to pay 300 dollars! Of course, there was the promise that the mercenary would be free from persecution and that when he died he would go straight to Heaven, which is quite a contract!' This was not the most encouraging start to their work, but there were many openings for preaching in spite of resistance from the Establishment, which no doubt stiffened their will.

*

The first any worker heard of Campo Hermoso Evangelicals was when they sought help from the nearest missionary. The Church in Campo Hermoso, in the vast rugged southern region of the Department of Tolima high in the Central Andes, sprang up spontaneously.

When the government opened areas on both sides of the Central Cordillera for housing, Zoilo Torres, Elias Gongora and several other families decided to move from Cundinamarca, between Bogota and the Magdalena River, where they were labourers on large estates, and secure land for themselves. They settled on the eastern slopes of the Central Cordillera between 5,000 and 7,000 feet in good coffee country. They cut down jungle and started their cattle farms and coffee planatations. One day on a 'food run' to town to buy supplies, they found the salt wrapped in a copy of the *Mensaje Evangelico*, published by Carlos Chapman of the Gospel Missionary Union in Cali. On the back of this four-page sheet they saw a list of books – New Testaments, Bibles, and other Christian literature. They wrote to Cali and ordered one each of the books, after travelling for several days to the nearest post-office.

Eventually the books reached them and they started reading. Each of these pioneers became an ardent Evangelical and soon others in the district were converted. At this time it was not even a village but a huge rural area spread out against mountains and named El Platanal. The farmer Zoilo Torres was believed by the community to be divinely annointed and they appointed him their spiritual leader. They never heard a preacher or evangelist, but met at first in each other's houses for worship, using the words of hymns from the books they had ordered to tunes of their own invention.

*

In Armenia the Taylors were in need of help so they decided to hold discipleship classes between the times of the coffee harvest. Two or three of the most promising young men were to be invited to attend to train as self-supporting evangelists. The three the Taylors finally chose included Martinez, who took time off from his carpenter's shop to attend the course held for eight hours a day over a period of ten days.

The young men then returned to their normal labours and joined Clyde Taylor to campaign at weekends. 'This gave me an opportunity to speak, for them to listen and learn, and also to give their testimony. The outcome was that in two or three years, these men – and a woman recruited the following year – turned out to be the best workers we ever had.'

When the sponsoring society, the Christian and Missionary Alliance, saw the results the Taylors were getting from training these young evangelists, it was decided they were the right people to found a Bible school. So in 1934, Clyde Taylor and his wife started a short-term Bible college, which offered a modern 'sandwich course'. Three months of study were followed by three months 'in the field', with time provided for students either to work and earn their tuition or to teach and preach.

The school was co-educational and at once started training young women to be elementary schoolteachers. Illiteracy in the area was high, and the Taylors knew from experience that 'you cannot establish effective Churches without literate Christians'.

Dr. Taylor had some regrets about starting a bible school at this time 'because we stopped seeking followers and started educating people.

'I am convinced that you can do both at the same time but we were carrying too heavy a load. Not only were we responsible for the Bible school but also for the many congregations that were springing up across the Quindio Valley.'

Despite his misgivings about neglecting their evangelism, at the end of ten years they had a hundred preaching points all over the huge Quindio Valley. Much of the work was carried on by itinerant workers of the Bible school, who spent much of their time visiting scattered congregations, to preach the gospel and to strengthen the believers.

Clyde Taylor decided that the growing bible school must have its own buildings. They were put up by faith and Martinez, but the faith came first. The Mission organizers were short of money during the Depression and they gave permission to put up the buildings only so long as the men on the spot found the money. 'The land came in one large gift which was the answer to prayer and an indication that God was with us,' says Clyde Taylor. 'After that money came in smaller and larger amounts, mostly from people we did not know.'

Martinez agreed to oversee the labourers. He closed his carpenter's shop and worked full-time for the project, although, as well as acting as foreman, he continued his studies and was active as a lay preacher.

Clyde Taylor remembers how Martinez proved his craftsmanship and ingenuity in the enterprise. 'We had wood-working machinery that was meant to be portable and not to be put to heavy work, and so we improvised all kinds of gadgets to refine this machinery. Martinez did virtually all the machine work, the processing of lumber that we needed for flooring and the making of windows and doors.' He went on, 'Every Friday, Martinez and I would meet to determine if we could pay our labourers for the following week because we had to let them know every pay-day whether we could use them the next week or not.'

One of the most dramatic answers to prayer came when the missionaries needed roof tiles for the larger building. They had estimated it would cost 1,500 dollars to put the roof on, but the mail came in and there was no money.

'We were afraid we were going to be in real trouble,' recalls Clyde Taylor. 'Not only would we have to dismiss our labour force but the rainy season was coming and we *needed* that roof on. There was not much sense in going to the post-office on a Friday morning because normally there was no mail in that day. But I went. There was just one letter in the box and when I opened it I found a cheque for 1,500 dollars. It turned out that the post-office had sent the letter to the wrong address and it had been delayed a couple of days. The Lord really wanted to try our faith! I went to the building where Martinez was working and told him the news. I can still hear him yell "Halleluya!" '

The first building was started in 1937 and the second and larger building the next year. At a ceremony on the new campus in 1939 Martinez was one of the first three students to graduate, and by that time the two main buildings were finished and classes were being held in them.

After Martinez graduated, he took charge of the Alliance Church in Armenia, ministering to his congregation in a rented hall, until the Mission could buy a building there, their first church property. He appeared to have a special gift of healing, not by the laying on of hands, but through his prayers. Clyde Taylor heard of many instances of sick people cured after the pastor had prayed for them.

*

In the Central Cordillera the gospel spread quickly and Zoilo Torres, whom the people had made their spiritual leader, gave the name of Campo Hermoso to the area originally called El Platanal. The words mean 'beautiful field', and he explained, 'Although the mountain range is rugged, the region is like a beautiful field where the gospel is sowing its seeds of peace.'

In Campo Hermoso the influence of the gospel was powerful. Disagreements never reached the local courts because the religious leaders, or the Church Council, settled them in a brotherly way. Christ ruled there and the remote 'diocese' was a privileged place.

In 1934 Torres gave a plot of his land on top of a knoll to the burgeoning Church, and the people of Campo Hermoso laboured to build their own chapel to hold a hundred worshippers. The next year it was pulled down and a larger one built in its place.

The first the missionaries heard of the Christians of Campo Hermoso was when they wrote to the Rev. Carlos Chapman, of the Gospel Missionary Union in Cali, asking for someone to baptize their first believers. He put them in touch with the Christian and Missionary Alliance who sent the Rev. Henry Fast from Neiva, Huila. Mr. Fast held the first baptismal service and helped to organize the church formally.

After his visit this remote congregation really started to grow. They tithed their money and produce, and each leader gave a tithe of his time to go out and spread the gospel. The reach of the Church spread for miles in every direction. The first Church Council was formed led by Torres and his brothers, and a school was opened with the help of students from the new Bible Institute in Armenia.

By 1938 it was decided to build yet a larger chapel, the third in four years, to hold 500 worshippers. The congregation had multiplied by five, although to be an Evangelical Christian in those challenging days and in this wild country was totally and dangerously committing. Each one became an 'apostle', and with the help of a few preachers the work grew to encompass a huge 'parish'.

Missionary visits continued every six months, but the church was run mostly by lay workers until 1944 when a graduate from the Bible Institute in Armenia, Moises Manchola, was in charge, and Pastor Martinez led the congregation occasionally. In the spring of 1950, he was asked to take the pastorate of the church in Campo Hermoso.

*

After the martyrdom of Pastor Martinez, George Constance helped to reorganize the church council at Campo Hermoso and made plans to renew their pastoral activities. Yet the lull in the violence was only the prelude to a fiercer storm. Marauding mobs again invaded the region destroying and burning. The few houses that remained were burnt down and so were the granaries. Cattle were stolen and many civilians wounded and tortured.

There was a general exodus to the mountains where the people lived for three years, sheltering in caves and under trees. Mostly they lived on wild fruit and roots, occasionally supplemented by small rations obtained by taking great risks. Epidemics, hunger and cold brought the deaths of more than 800 adults and at least a thousand children.

Gradually both the political and religious strife subsided. By the mid-fifties the refugee families in Campo Hermoso began to return to their ruined homes and spoiled livelihoods. A forlorn landscape spread out before them where ten years earlier had been prosperous coffee plantations and cattle farms. There was not one head of cattle in an enormous area and most of the buildings were burned to the ground. The hard-working and courageous people began to rebuild. Once again the farm fields sprouted with seedlings and their churches and ministries grew strong. For the fourth time they built a chapel on the knoll at Campo Hermoso, and in 1955 a school was opened. The strength of the Evangelical Christians increased many times. Martinez' widow, Maria, returned to Armenia to teach.

The Bible Institute in Armenia, started by Clyde Taylor and his wife, is now called the Bethel Bible Institute and is a training centre to prepare pastors and evangelists for the whole of Colombia. Today there is a splendid new campus with modern buildings and many students. The Christian and Missionary Alliance now has about a hundred pastors in Colombia with a total church membership of about eight thousand.

Campo Hermoso continues to justify the martyrdom of Martinez and to fulfil the hopes of Toilo Zorres who had christened it 'a beautiful field' for harvesting the gospel.

Maximilian Kolbe

1894–1941

Some Christians have sought martyrdom by violent means, taking their own lives, or by the deliberate provocation of those who killed them. No death in these circumstances can be venerated as martyrdom. When Maximilian Kolbe, Polish priest and a Franciscan, invited the Nazis to kill him, it was in exchange for the life of another man. He volunteered for death in obedience to Christ's commandment, 'Love one another, as I have loved you. Greater love hath no man than this, that a man lay down his life for his friends.'

In his manner of dying he is unlike other martyrs in this book although his martyrdom is none the less valid. Christian martyrs are those who die because they refuse to renounce the Christian faith, or to disobey any law or command of the Church.

Oswiecim, an industrial town in the Province of Cracow in Southern Poland, where the Vistula and Iola Rivers meet, attracted worldwide notoriety for the Nazi concentration camp established nearby in 1940, Auschwitz. The name still harrows the imagination of the world, for no fewer than four million people were massacred there. Auschwitz was a place where simply to be shot dead was a kindness.

The Oswiecim State Museum, built on the site in 1946, is a Memorial to those who died. One of the four million, Prisoner Number 16670, was a priest, Maximilian Kolbe, who gave his life for a fellow-inmate. Ten men were condemned to a starvation bunker as a reprisal for an escaper; and Father Kolbe chose to die in place of Sergeant Francis Gajowniczek, who had a wife and children. The young soldier survived the camp, and he and his wife are still alive and living in Brzeg on the Odra in the west of Poland; but their two sons died during the Warsaw Uprising of 1944 before their father was released.

On October 17, 1971, the 54th anniversary of the founding of his Militia which was to spread its influence across the world, Maximilian Kolbe was declared Blessed by Pope Paul VI in the

Basilica of St. Peter in Rome before a vast concourse of sixty thousand people from many nations. Among them was Francis Gajowniczek.

*

He was born Raymond Kolbe on January 8, 1894, the fourth of five sons, two of whom died in infancy. His parents, Jules and Maria, were hard-working Polish weavers, and both devoted to the Church. As a girl Maria had a religious vocation, but under the Third Partition of Poland in 1875 the largest part of the country fell to the Russians who suppressed the convents.

His father was a diffident man and Maria ruled the household. She was a determined woman who insisted that boys needed both love and discipline, but Raymond was unrepressed by his mother's severity. He was stubborn, independent, and mischievous with a volatile temperament, and tested her patience constantly.

One day, pushed to the limits of vexation, she scolded him, 'My poor child, what will become of you?' Her words were commonplace rhetoric, but they caught the imagination of the disobedient small boy. He began to pray before the little family altar of Our Lady of Czestochowa. He became submissive, quiet; and he often looked as if he had been crying. With motherly concern Maria insisted that Raymond should tell her what was on his mind.

Tremulously the boy replied, 'When you said to me, "Whatever will become of you?" I felt very sad, and I asked the Blessed Virgin. She appeared to me, holding two crowns, one white, one red. She looked lovingly at me and asked me which one I would choose. The white one meant I would always be pure, the red one, I would die a martyr. I answered, "I choose both of them." She smiled and disappeared.'

*

To augment the money she and her husband earned as weavers, Maria Kolbe started a corner shop, supplying the humble wants of her neighbours – herrings, sauerkraut, garlic, candles and shoelaces – and she also worked as a midwife. Raymond, a versatile and willing lad, soon learnt to help in the shop, and cooked for the family when his mother was called to a nursing case.

The Kolbes were struggling hard to keep their eldest son,

Francis, at a business school in Pabianice, near the textile centre of Lodz, because there was no free education under the Russians. Then Raymond seized the kind offer of a local pharmacist, Kotowski, to tutor him. By the end of a year he was level with his brother and his parents decided they must afford school for him too.

Four years after Raymond started school at Pabianice, both the Kolbe boys asked to be admitted to the Minor Seminary of Lwow, the capital of Galicia, which was the name given to the Polish territories annexed by Austria. Their parents, drawn to the religious life themselves, rejoiced despite the impending separation from their young sons. Jules Kolbe escorted them to Cracow, the oldest city of Poland and one of the best-preserved mediaeval cities in Europe, which was then in the Austrian zone. They crossed the frontier secretly, as Poles often did, and at Cracow Jules bade his sons godspeed. Alone on their adventure, the boys took the horse and cart to Lwow.

At the Minor Seminary Raymond, aged thirteen, astonished and frequently challenged his Franciscan tutors with his exceptional ability in mathematics and the sciences. Later he planned interplanetary flights and designed machines to reach the moon. He also had a passion for war games, involving tactical skills. One day in a local park he devised a system of fortifications which would render Lwow impregnable to attack, inventing a sophisticated chessboard as a battleground and using bits of wood as pawns. He was a born soldier, mesmerized by the military life, and it took a second spiritual crisis to deter him from this profession.

When Raymond reached the age of sixteen, he needed to decide if he would enter the novitiate, and he determined to pluck up moral courage to tell the Father Provincial that he did not feel he had a call to the religious life. Before he could do so he was summoned to the visitors' parlour. His mother had called at the Friary with momentous news. Following in the footsteps of Francis and Raymond, the third son, Joseph, had decided to become a religious. Moreover, both she and Jules had decided to fulfil a lifelong ambition and enter the service of religion. Jules had already gone to Cracow to the Franciscan Friars, and she was joining the Benedictine Sisters at Lwow.

When his mother proudly announced, 'Now all the family

works for God,' Raymond found it impossible to blurt out his intention. He began to waver. Was he merely pampering his wishes to be a soldier? What did God want him for? Suddenly his own vocation became crystal clear and when his mother went joyfully on her way, he *ran* to the Father Provincial to request the Franciscan religious habit. Raymond was dead; Maximilian was born. He took the name of the Saint who suffered martyrdom in the third century for refusing to be a soldier.

*

Maximilian Kolbe pronounced his temporary vows in 1911 and in the autumn of the following year he was told to attend the Gregorian University in Rome. The opportunity to study at the heart of Christendom would surely have enraptured most novices but at first Maximilian was perplexed, even scandalized by the prospect. Apparently he equated Rome with loose women who accosted even monks in the streets. As a realist and a handsome young man of eighteen, his immediate reaction was to flee from temptation! He would forego the glorious religious ambience of Rome rather than endanger the visionary white crown of purity which he had been proffered. But holy obedience to which he was pledged cannot choose.

All his life obedience was his invincible weapon. He obeyed his superiors unswervingly without even mild discussion. It is an awesome responsibility to determine the will of God for another, and knowing Maximilian to be unreservedly docile, and perfectly obedient, they were cautious in giving him instructions.

In his letters from Rome to his mother he never wrote about himself, but there were unmistakable signs of his spiritual growth, an enriched inner life. His feet were on the lower steps of the steep ladder to saintliness. His Eastertide greetings to his mother (April 6, 1914) make abundantly clear the rigid programme of spiritual life he had charted for himself. He wrote with passion, 'I will wish you neither health nor prosperity. Why? Because I want to wish you better than that, something so good that God would not wish you better: that in all things, the will of this very good Father be accomplished in you, that you may know in all things how to fulfil the will of God. This is the very best I can wish for you. God himself could not wish better than that.'

On November 1, All Saints Day 1914, Friar Maximilian took the solemn vows of a Franciscan. At the International College of the Order, in San Teodoro Street, fringing the Palatine, the community followed anxiously the war communiqués. Friar Maximilian's Polish colleagues, who were all Austrian subjects, had to leave Italy upon the outbreak of war, but he had a Russian passport and was allowed to stay.

*

Friar Maximilian was a paradox: both a man of action and a contemplative; a prayerful man and a visionary, but also a pragmatist and a technocrat. He passed his examinations with brilliance – he was a doctor of philosophy at twenty-one and four years later passed his doctorate in sacred theology. At the same time he persevered in the harder task, simply to live the Beatitudes. Constantly he was striving for perfection, telling himself that every day must mean greater holiness. 'I must become the greatest possible saint,' he resolved.

In the summer of 1917 he was stricken by illness and diagnosed consumptive, but making light of the haemorrhages and headaches, he started a project which was to become the legacy of his life. He decided that this was the time, when all the powers of evil were let loose by the Great War, to start a Society, whose members would become a company of saints.

This resolution was strengthened by the sacrilegious conduct of the fiercely anti-clerical Freemasons in Rome in 1917, while they were celebrating the second centenary of their organization. Some of the blasphemous charades of the Freemasons made a strong impression on the young friars of the Palatine, who at an exhibition in St. Peter's Plaza saw for themselves fanatics flourishing outrageous slogans. One read, 'Satan must reign in the Vatican! The Pope will be his slave!' Friar Maximilian saw the Freemasons waving banners under the Vatican windows showing the devil trampling on St. Michael. When they started to distribute vicious tracts against the Pope, the idea came to him of recruiting his own spiritual army 'to fight the evils of the day'.

In the face of such strong attacks by the enemies of the Church of God it was not enough simply to complain and weep. He wrote, 'Let us remember that at the Divine Judgement we will have to give a strict account not only of the things we have done, but also of all the good works which we might have performed but have negligently left undone. Each of us bears the obligation to stand in the trenches and bare our breast to the onslaught of the enemy.'

His first action was to ask the Rector's permission to go to the Palazzo Verde, the offices of the Freemasons, to convert the Grand Master himself. The Rector told his young crusader that it was perhaps too much to expect for the present, and suggested it would be better to start by praying for the conversion of the Freemasons. Friar Maximilian did so at once.

Then, with the permission of the Father Rector, the first meeting of Maximilian's Society was held on October 17, 1917, at night behind the closed doors of an inner cell. The only stipulations were that the members should pledge total personal consecration to Mary Immaculate, to be used by her as an instrument for the conquest of the world for Christ, and that they should wear the international symbol of the Mary Immaculate medal, known as the 'miraculous medal'. (This medal was struck in 1830 after the Venerable Catherine Labouré, Sister of Charity of St. Vincent de Paul, claimed its design had been given to her in three visions of the Blessed Virgin Mary that year, Our Lady appeared to her standing on a globe and bearing a globe, with rays of light coming from her hands. Catherine, who was canonized in 1947, was commanded on the second and third occasions to have a medal struck after the model revealed, and a promise of 'great graces ' was made to those who wear it when blessed.) The work aimed to make available to everybody the happiness that comes from the presence of God, the first source of all happiness. Internationally the Society became known as Militia Immaculatae; in America, The Knights of the Immaculate, and in Britain, The Crusade of the Immaculate.

The seven founder members were: Father Joseph Pal, priest of the Roumanian province; Father Anthony Glowinski, deacon of the Roumanian province; Friar Jerome Biasi of the Paduan province; Father Quirico Pignalberi of the Roman province; Friar Anthony Mansi and Friar Henry Granata, both of the Neapolitan province; and Friar Maximilian himself, of the province of Padua.

They obtained the Pope's verbal blessing through Bishop Dominic Jacquet of the Franciscan Order, but for more than a year after the inaugural meeting the Militia Immaculatae made no progress. The seven did not have equal faith in its future, and one even tried to undermine the belief of the others by saying that 'none of them had much sense'!

Soon after the formation of the Militia, Maximilian had a relapse in health and during his break from studies, copied out a programme for the Society to deliver to the Father General, Dominic Tavani, asking for his written blessing. Their main activities then were prayer and the distribution of the 'miraculous medals'. The Father General wrote a blessing and expressed his desire to spread the Militia among the Catholic youth. He added wistfully, 'If only there were twelve of you . . .' (Francis of Assisi and his followers had numbered twelve when they went to Rome in 1209 to ask permission to start a brotherhood). After the Father General made this remark, new members joined in great numbers. This was just as well, for Maximilian Kolbe saw his enterprise on no small scale and planned global conquests. The Jesuit motto is 'Ad majorem Dei gloriam' – 'For the greater glory of God.' His was 'For the *greatest* glory of God'. Only the superlative would suffice. His apostolic zeal recognized no boundaries: he wanted to convert all sinners everywhere as fast as possible. He had no idea of establishing a devout élite nor did he wish to restrict his movement to the Franciscan Order. He saw the Knights spreading among all religious congregations, all Orders. Christianity knows no frontiers and his field of evangelism was the world. He professed to love even the Germans; he practised love for his enemies as the essence of the Christian religion.

*

On April 28, 1918, in a beautiful Roman springtime, Friar Maximilian was ordained priest. Now he was 'fully armed'. He was often teased for his love of military terms, and once wrote, 'The morning meditation is the plan of battle for the entire day, while the examination of conscience is the review of the ordeal of that battlefield.' He would say sweepingly, 'We will put the large pieces of artillery in motion,' and he liked to talk of his 'engines of war'.

Maximilian embraced new developments enthusiastically and strove to transform them into 'weapons of conquest'. When motion pictures began to appear some of his brothers greeted them as 'instruments of ruin'. 'Satan and his agents take possession of all the inventions to convert them to evil,' they protested. But Kolbe gave a stalwart reply, 'All the more reason to get to work to reconquer the positions taken by the enemy.' The press loomed large in his mind as a big gun in the Catholic armoury, and he cherished plans for a magazine to preach the gospel to all nations.

After his ordination, in one of his last letters to his mother before she died, Maximilian wrote, 'Pray for me, so that my love may grow more and more quickly and without any limit. *Pray especially that it will be without limits.*'

The new priest returned to Poland plagued again by tuberculosis in July 1919. He was at once made a professor at the Franciscan Friary at Cracow, and there established a group of Knights drawn from theology students of the friars' seminary. He also organized groups for the friar priests and the 'Gentiles', as he liked to term the lay people. Meetings were held each month and the number of candidates increased daily.

Less than six months later Father Maximilian became so debilitated that in the summer of 1920 his superiors sent him to the sanatorium at Zakopane, the tourist resort at the foot of the Polish Carpathians. Here he was surrounded by unbelievers. He lost little time in engaging in controversy and had no difficulty in fighting the freethinkers on their own ground because he was well-read in science as well as philosophy.

His own persistent illness gave him an empathy with the sick and he welcomed 'his Sister Suffering' with real Franciscan joy. He was adamant, 'All these trials are useful, necessary, and even indispensable, like the crucible where gold is purified.' In a speech to clerics on November 15, 1919, he even went so far as to describe suffering as 'not only useful, but desirable'. He declared, 'We will do very much more if we are plunged into exterior and interior darkness, filled with sorrow, weakened, exhausted, without consolation, persecuted at each step, surrounded by continual failures, abandoned by all, ridiculed, scoffed at as was Jesus on the Cross; provided that we pray with all our strength for those who persecute us and provided that we want by all means to draw them to God'. He was to put it more simply, and poignantly, in a letter to brother clerics at Lwow in 1933, 'My dear brothers, how very short life really is . . . How swiftly time passes us by . . . The more sufferings the better, for after death we can no longer suffer. Time is short to prove our love, and we live but once.'

Membership of the Militia was now growing fast and Father Maximilian decided he would publish a Review to keep members in touch with him and with each other. He steeled himself to beg for the money he needed and the first issue of *The Knight of the Immaculate* appeared in January 1922. It was a time when devaluation in Poland was bankrupting the best-established publications and after the second edition he could not pay the printer. The Guardian of the Friary reproved him with an old Polish proverb, 'This is what happens, my son, when you try to attack the moon with a spade!' After Mass the impoverished editor found an envelope on the altar containing the exact amount of the printer's bill.

Of course he had his critics. People objected that St. Francis founded the Order to produce men who would preach and hear confessions, not become publishers and businessmen. Father Maximilian did not attempt to defend himself. He was too busy putting his case for a printing press to the Father Provincial.

The reply was that he could have a press if he found the money for it. A visiting American priest, fired by Maximilian's vision, donated a hundred dollars, and it was not long before the new editor had enough money to buy an ancient printing press from the Sisters of Divine Mercy at Lagiewniki, near Cracow. He christened it 'Old Grandmother'. It took all a man's strength to run – 60,000 turns were needed to print the 5,000 copies of the Review. Unconcerned by its decrepitude Maximilian saw its arrival as a splendid start; he was determined the press was going to be an efficient instrument of the apostolate in the modern world.

His superiors lived in dread of Father Maximilian's next fantastic scheme and found decidedly uncomfortable the onus he put on them as arbiters of 'holy obedience'. They were also getting complaints from the fathers at Cracow whose tranquil, almost mediaeval, life-style had been so rudely disrupted by the machine age. So they hit upon a tidy solution. Father Maximilian was to go to Grodno, a northern port on the Neman River near the border of Lithuania, to carry on his printing activities. A large but decrepit

Friary there could spare three rooms for his enterprise. The superiors convinced themselves that they were not sending him into the wilderness, but were thinking only of his health and could, with clear consciences, recommend the beneficial climate of this old oriental city.

When Father Maximilian arrived at Grodno on October 20, 1922, he found little support or understanding of his purposes among the aged friars who had retired there. He was let off none of his normal duties and at first had only two helpers working on the Review. But Maximilian was a born leader who attracted devoted assistants and soon the few priests at the monastery were greatly outnumbered by the printers who became Franciscan brothers. He was adamant that they should all be treated alike and so traditional routines were upset.

The circulation of the Review now increased to such an extent that the brothers could not keep abreast of demand. The sincerity and enthusiasm of the editor, Maximilian, brought him more and more readers who begged for back issues and borrowed numbers to copy. He wrote most of the Review himself, logically and plainly for the ordinary people, the poor Polish masses, who were eager to read his simple exposition of the truths of the faith. His policy was clear-cut, to produce the Review cheaply and in large quantities. 'A worthwhile and reasonably priced book will find many buyers,' he said. 'A working person does not have time to read trash.' His short apologetical articles in dialogue form were an object lesson in effective communication. The Review aimed to present doctrine, recall catechism, and deepen the devotion of the Polish people to the Immaculate.

Maximilian also possessed sound business acumen. He found it fruitful propaganda, for example, to send the Review free of charge to anyone who asked, because this prompted many subscribers to pay for those who could not afford copies. He would not accept advertisements; space was too valuable for spiritual teaching; but in one issue he published photographs of the brothers in religious habit 'putting the paper to bed', i.e. preparing it for printing. This was a new picture of the religious life for many people, and at once attracted more recruits to work for him. Maximilian also gave scrupulous attention to the answering of readers' letters, which presented the opportunity 'to direct souls'.

This he saw as work of immeasurable importance and, he counselled his workers, 'One needs to pray a great deal for one's readers, and that one might serve them well.'

This form of the apostolate was proving so successful within a year that his superiors ordered that an entire wing of the Grodno monastery should be turned into a printing house. Now that he had sufficient space Father Maximilian began to improve his tools and bought a saw machine and a diesel engine. The Review paid for much of it but he had a miraculous way of getting things he wanted at knock-down prices!

In three years both the number of brothers in the Militia and the circulation of the Review doubled. So impressed was the Provincial Father that he asked if he could be admitted as a Knight. But in 1926 Maximilian's health broke down again and he returned to Zakopane under orders not even to think about the printing concern. At Grodno his brother, Father Alphonus, a devotee who imitated him in every detail, deputized.

The paper continued to prosper; its circulation reached nearly half a million copies in 1926. The elderly and cautious friars now wanted to curb expansion and bank the income to provide for the Friary, but the idea was anathema to Father Maximilian who saw it as mistaking the means for the end. 'God forbid that we should ever have any large provisions in the cash-box, or maybe even income from investments,' he wrote. 'Our greatness is not to be found in amassing material things, but rather to be freed from them. The world says: "Blessed are the rich," but Jesus says, "Blessed are the poor." '

He returned from Zakopane to defend the rights of 'holy poverty'. The work should not become a comfortable lucrative enterprise; its purpose was to win the world for Christ. His poverty had a marvellously modern interpretation: the needs of the brothers must be of the most frugal (how else could the paper be produced so cheaply?); but for God and the Immaculate must be provided model workshops, streamlined super-efficient machinery, and the fastest transport. Unbelievers exploited new machines to make money. Why should Christians be afraid of turning them to the service of God? asked Maximilian.

*

However, it had become apparent by 1927 that a printing establishment could not co-exist with an ordinary Franciscan friary. The fathers complained that their religious observances were disrupted and the brothers found it difficult to work in a hostile atmosphere. In any case the enterprise had expanded so rapidly that it had outgrown its present quarters. Father Maximilian decided that it was imperative to move from Grodno and his Provincial encouraged him to find a place of his own.

By the summer of 1927 he had found land near Warsaw, where he could build 'The City of the Immaculate', a printing 'village'. This time, however, the Provincial refused permission, finding the condition of the offering of Masses in perpetuity too onerous. Of course, Father Maximilian submitted without argument, and told the owner, Prince Drucki Lubecki, that the transaction was off. Then the Prince was moved to give the land for nothing and the Provincial gave his blessing.

The first twenty friars left at once to put up workmen's huts on the site. Then they started building sheds for the printing presses. Local peasants brought them provisions and also lent helping hands. A holy alliance sprang out of sharing food and toil so that the people of the surrounding countryside came to call the place our 'Niepokalanow', which means 'the domain of the Immaculate'.

Miraculously, Father Maximilian kept well in spite of the heavy labour and scant sleep. He did not spare himself and was always the first at work. There is heartwarming testimony of the affection he lavished upon the 'little brothers' at this time. One wrote, 'I do not think that parents have ever loved their children so much, so providently and so tenderly.' It is true that Father Maximilian would often recommend the superiors to treat them 'maternally'. 'If they feel too tired they must have rest,' said their Guardian who laboured harder than any of them. It was no life of convenience he preached, and he realized that to help found Niepokalanow they had abandoned all, and sometimes at great sacrifice. 'They must then find in us a new family, a real one,' he insisted.

Father John Burdyszek, who was later to establish the English Crusade Centre in Manchester, worked for six years at Niepokalanow and speaks of the self-effacing leadership of the bearded priest. 'He would say to us "I am your Guardian but you can escape my eyes; I am not a spy – your superiors are God and Our Lady." He was a thin man with no colour in his face, but you could trace his soul in his eyes. When away on his travels he kept in touch continually by correspondence which gave the community their "spiritual food".'

From their new home new publications appeared and the most spectacular, a national newspaper, *Maly Dziennik* ('Little Journal') was launched in May 1935. At once it attracted a huge readership. The secular press was covetous. Circulations continued to fall in the economic depression, and popular newspapers 'folded'; while 'The Little Journal' thrived. Maximilian recruited professional journalists and the paper sold well because it was the cheapest 'national' in the country and the people liked its political neutrality. Its policy was to present world affairs fully and objectively. The journalists were lay, but apart from some of the professors in the Minor Seminary everyone else in the community was religious.

Although prayer always came before action and no one was allowed to forget the spiritual raison-d'etre of the work, there was nothing amateur about this printing enterprise. The holy workmen were outstanding technicians, highly trained and intelligent. Four of the linotype operators had the highest rating in Poland for setting type. There was a special box inviting 'Inventions and Projects', and Niepokalnow had several patents among its assets.

No partiality was shown between priests and brothers. There were, in fact, only six priests but more than seven hundred brothers, and only 'the beloved sick' were privileged. Father Maximilian always referred to the sick as 'my best fellow-workers' because they gave so much in prayer, and in this way helped them to overcome a feeling of uselessness.

Niepokalanow became a place for pilgrimage. It was considered a model industrial enterprise and its workers won renown for their sanctity. Niepokalanow had become a school for saints.

*

But in the grandiose schemes of Father Maximilian, Poland was only a springboard. Three years after founding 'The City' he decided upon a similar venture in Japan and won the approval of his Provincial. With four of the brothers the priest set out for Japan on February 26, 1930. He left two of the brothers at Shanghai to start a group of Knights there and he pressed on with the others to Nagasaki. They landed there on April 24.

A month later he cabled home, 'Today we are sending out our first issue. Have a printing establishment.' Bishop Hyasaki of Nagasaki was inclined to ridicule the proposal of the missionaries from Poland to publish a Review without proper backing. Then he discovered that Father Maximilian held two learned doctorates and invited him to give courses in his seminary. The Polish priest was swift to barter. 'Gladly, on the condition that you permit us to publish the Review,' he said. The bishop was won over, 'It's a bargain!'

Father Maximilian bought an old printing machine – 'very much like our old Grandmother!' – and his ambitions grew with the success of his efforts. He wrote home, 'As soon as our work is well established in Japan, I will leave to make foundations in India and afterwards at Beirut for the Arabs. I expect to publish the Review in Turkish, Persian, Arabic and Hebrew.'

Two months after his arrival in Japan Father Maximilian was summoned to attend the Provincial Chapter at Lwow to debate the future of the Japanese Mission. He returned to Japan on August 24 with authority to found a Japanese Niepokalanow and to open a novitiate for them. He went back just in time, because his absence so soon after initiating the enterprise had plunged things into chaos: the Review had not been published and the Mission was nearly broke.

It did not take Father Maximilian long to put things right and soon he was negotiating to buy land on a steep ridge fringing the city of Nagasaki on which to establish *Mugenzai No Sono* (The Garden of the Immaculate). This was opened there on May 16, 1931, and when the atomic bomb was dropped in 1954, 'The Garden' was virtually unscathed and no one killed. Was it because of the protected position of the site?

In a letter to his Polish brothers written while at Nagasaki Maximilian outlined his strategy for countering militant atheism. 'It is essential to study these anti-religious movements in a positive spirit because they also contain something good, and it is the duty of the Christian apostle to find these good elements and incorporate them in his own teaching and action.' Father Maximilian

was convinced that it was because Christians had failed to practise the principles they professed, or apply them to the needs of
their own time, that Christianity had suffered many defeats in the
contemporary world.

In 1933 Father Maximilian left for India, stopping at Singapore
to make preparations for a Malayan Review. In India he hastened
to Ernakulam where the Catholic Archbishop lived, but his reception was chilly and unpromising. So he prayed before the statue of
St. Thérèse of Lisieux in the passage of the Archbishopric. A rose
petal fell at his feet from a vase at the base of the statue and he
construed this as a promise of help from the little saint. He was
not the least surprised when all the obstructions from the ecclesi-
astical authorities in India were smoothed out and the Archbishop
wrote formally inviting the Polish missionaries of the Order to
proceed. But unhappily, Father Maximilian was not there to hurry
the preparations and the friars delayed because of the rumblings
of war.

By this time he was again a very sick man, and was recalled to
Poland in May 1936. As always he obeyed without demur, although his heart remained with his 'dear pagans' in foreign
missions.

Now he tackled all his work with a profound urgency, as if
aware that the time left to him was brief. In 1937 he introduced a
Five-Year Plan for Niepokalanow. The next year *The Little Knight*
began publication for young people. The national newspaper, *The
Little Journal*, was printed in eleven daily editions. He began *Miles
Immaculatae*, a Latin quarterly for priests, and opened SP3RN –
Polish Station 3 Radio Niepokalanow. In the spring of 1939 he
went to Lithuania to prepare for a Lithuanian Niepokalanow in
Linkiewies, and sent a delegation to Belgium with the same objec-
tive.

Petitions asking him to start new Niepokalanows arrived from
all over the world. The membership in the Militia was now nearly
one million and the circulation of the Review exceeeded this
figure. On the eve of the Second World War Father Maximilian
had begun to build an airport and four runways at Niepokalanow,
and he was also hoping to produce Catholic films. He was a truly
modern missionary.

*

As war seemed inevitable, Father Maximilian made one of his rare personal confidences to a group of his confrères. Shyly, but earnestly, he told them that while he had been in Japan 'Heaven was promised to me in all certitude.' 'I am so happy, my heart overflows with peace and joy.'

He was anxious both to prepare his brothers for the cruelties of war and to reassure them of their own spiritual safety. 'I want you to know, my brothers, that an atrocious conflict is brewing. In our beloved Poland we must expect the worst.' But, he insisted, 'Exterior and interior sufferings can serve only to sanctify us. Our condition is such that no one nor anything can do us harm . . . *We are invincible.*'

He made explicit his thoughts on martyrdom at this time. 'Would it not be the supreme honour if we could seal our faith with our blood?' he asked. 'During the first few centuries the Church was persecuted. The blood of martyrs watered the seeds of Christianity. Later, when the persecutions ceased, one of the Fathers of the Church deplored the lukewarmness of Christians. He rejoiced when persecutions returned. In the same way we must rejoice in what will happen, for in the midst of trials our zeal will become more ardent.'

He insisted that in persecution the power of God is shown more clearly, 'that power which cannot be broken'. Speaking of the victory of martyrs over their persecutors, he told the brothers, 'Martyrdom is a service. At most they can take our lives. Then they will render us the greatest service of all so we will be able to grasp our murderers with both hands by the scalp, or rather by the heart, so that they will take our places here on earth.'

Maximilian reminded them that it was only after the persecution in Jerusalem and the departure from that city of the first Christians into other parts of Palestine, that the teaching of Jesus spread. 'And with us it could be the same. It would be bad if someone himself placed himself in peril, for then God would not be obliged to help such a soul. But when he himself sends the circumstances, why then for us it is a special grace.'

He went on, 'When one wants to get the fish moving in the water, it is useful to send down a pike. The same is true in religious communities. If there were no persecutions, there would be a standstill. God permits that there will be an enemy so that we do not become slothful or lose the spirit of heroism.'

From the beginning of the war Niepokalanow was frequently bombed and Father Maximilian sent many of the brothers home to their families.

On September 1, 1939, German motorcycle troops roared up to the doors of the Friary and ordered those brothers who remained to leave at once. Only two were left to attend sick brothers and refugees and the rest were forced into cattle trucks to be taken to the camp at Amtiz. The place was not then a concentration camp, but the friars were ill-treated and ill-fed, deprived of warmth and any privacy. Father Maximilian's presence was their consolation. 'Courage, my children . . . let us learn how to profit from suffering . . . the end is in sight,' he would say.

Worse treatment followed in Pawiak prison in Warsaw, where in an attempt to make him renounce his faith, Father Maximilian was beaten and kicked unconscious.

From Pawiak prison they returned to Niepokalanow on the Feast of the Immaculate Conception (December 8) to find it had been ransacked but not destroyed. Gradually about half of the community came back, although the editorial staff especially were compelled to stay in hiding. Under their Guardian's instructions the brothers prayed fervently without ceasing, day and night, succeeding each other before the humble altar; but Father Maximilian was also a redoubtable man of action. He succeeded in publishing his Review even under German domination. It appeared once, on the same Feast day in 1940.

In it he wrote, 'No one in the world can change truth. What we can do and should do is to seek truth and serve it when we have found it.' The war with the Nazis revolved round lies; the lie of the superiority of the 'master race', the inferiority of the Jews, the victory of violence. 'Not even the most powerful propaganda machine in the world can change truth. The real conflict is an inner conflict. Beyond armies of occupation, unrestrained passions and the hecatombs of extermination camps, there are two irreconcilable enemies in the depth of every soul: good and evil, sin and love. And what use are the victories on the battlefield if we ourselves are defeated in our innermost personal selves?'

*

On February 17, 1941, a black car, looking like a hearse and bearing the death's-head insignia of the Gestapo arrived at the Friary. Father Maximilian was arrested with four other priests and taken back to Amtiz on the way to Auschwitz. Twenty friars at Niepokalanow offered themselves as hostages to replace their Guardian at Auschwitz. The Nazis refused permission but in any case it is inconceivable that Father Maximilian would have agreed to the plan. He never allowed himself privileges, even refusing a glass of tea in the Camp Infirmary because the other patients had none.

Oswiecim-Auschwitz was the place of further torture. Priests especially were vilified and victimized. They were called 'priest-swine', horse-whipped and given the heaviest work.

For two weeks Father Maximilian withstood the most savage treatment under a superintendent the prisoners called Krott the Bloody. Once, when the sickly priest stumbled carrying tree trunks, Krott ordered him fifty lashes. After this punishment had been meted out, Krott pushed him into a hollow in the wood and left him for dead. Later the priest rallied, and by night was carried back to the camp hospital by his friends. Here the sick died without medical care or attention of any sort. Father Maximilian, ignoring threats and commands, heard confessions throughout the night and comforted the dying.

A fellow inmate has testified to his behaviour in the camp. He did not lose his mildness of spirit. 'Always straightforward and uncomplicated in his manner of doing things, decided in everything, he was full of gentle humour and by his attitude he sustained others ... At whatever time of the day or night I went to him, there were sick people near his bed, listening to his consoling words and his teaching. "Everything ends," he said, "so sufferings too must end. The way to glory is the way of the cross." ' The prisoner said that Maximilian knew how to reply to the burning question of human sufferings, which, in the light of Christian idealism, are permitted by God for the purifying of religious life and the drawing out from it of a greater good.

After a fortnight Father Maximilian was sent to the invalids' block where he was exempt from work but received only half rations and these he often gave away. Here he risked more punishment by preaching his last sermons before a pathetic congregation of starving and wasted men. Before long he was discharged as an invalid and transferred to Block 14.

*

Camp Commandant Fritsch announced his dreadful decision at evening roll-call. 'The prisoner has not been found. Ten of you from his Block will die for him in the starvation bunker.' All day long pallid, staring, emaciated men had stood in the punishing sun while the others from different blocks went to work. Many had collapsed and the dead lay heaped in a pyramid. Fritsch walked down the lines in the huge parade ground and chose the condemned with sadistic relish. He flicked his cane, almost playfully, 'This one ... that one.' His deputy, Vice-Commandant Palitsch, recorded the prisoners' numbers which replaced all names at Auschwitz.

One of the men singled out for this most appalling death broke into sobs for his wife and children.

Suddenly a wraith-like figure broke ranks and miraculously was able to speak to the German Commandant without being instantly shot. 'I would like to die in place of one of the men you have condemned,' said Father Maximilian. His voice was barely audible. 'Why?' barked Fritsch. The priest was subtle in his reply, taking account of the canon of German rule which preferred to liquidate the weak and the old first. 'I am old and good for nothing,' he said (he was 47 years old). The uncomprehending German officer grasped almost gratefully at this bit of 'logic' in the priest's barter. He ordered Palitsch to alter the list of condemned prisoners' numbers and Sergeant Gajowniczek fell out.

The pathetic group shuffled off towards the starvation bunker in the light of a majestic sunset. 'You'll dry up like tulips,' mocked an SS gaoler. 'You'll get nothing to eat. Nothing to drink.' First made to strip naked, they descended into their black hell, the Guardian of Niepolankanow bringing up the rear, with spiritual rod and staff. He would die with them, giving solace to each one. The infernal cell, which before had rung with howls more animal than human, became a holy chapel. The thin voices of those who were to die lifted in hymns and praises.

On August 14, 1941, Father Maximilian was the last to die. The gaolers, frightened by the profound composure of the Catholic priest, hastened the end by injecting him with carbolic acid.

*

Today Blessed Maximilian has his 'armies' of two million 'troops' spread out strategically all over the world. In the communist countries the printing activities have been largely suppressed but Niepokalanow in Poland has now become a shrine with a huge basilica built as a testimony to the love of Maximilian. This is the new field of apostolic work for the community which now comprises 30 fathers, 190 friars and about 100 candidates. It also continues its evangelism by correspondence, popular missions and the propaganda of the 'miraculous medals'. All the printing machinery was confiscated by Nazis and Communists.

The Japanese Niepokalanow has changed its name to Seibo No Kishi (Knights of the Immaculate) and there are numerous branches which have become religious communities in all parts of Japan. The principle activities at Seibo No Kishi at Nagasaki are publishing and education. The community publishes religious books as well as magazines and bulletins and there are also schools on the site. Pilgrims come to the village to pray in the new church and before the Grotto of the Madonna of Lourdes.

Marytown became the national centre in America in 1974, and after the Director-General of the Militia, Father Giorgio Domanski, visited this Kolbean outpost recently, he wrote, 'It reminds me of the Polish Niepokalanow. A group of buildings on a vast tract of land, transformed from a farm, houses the religious – two fathers and fourteen friars – who run their own editorial office and press. Everywhere poverty and simplicity reign. There's a tremendous industry united to an intense spirit of prayer including the perpetual admiration of the Blessed Sacrament day and night – and to think that we are in America!'

In England the National Crusade Centre is in Manchester where it was first introduced in 1952 by Father John Burdyszek. Here the main work is the publishing of Crusade literature. The priests also preach and organize pilgrimages to Walsingham, Lourdes and Fatima. Father John is now director of a Polish House for the Aged, Our Lady's Centre at Laxton Hall, Corby. He also runs a parish, and looks after a permanent exhibition on the life of

Blessed Maximilian Kolbe. The new national director is Father Gerard McCann, who says that 20,000 families are members of The Crusade in England today.

Maximilian Kolbe claimed that the only criterion for advance of the Crusade was progress of the soul. He wrote at the outset of the second world war, 'Even if it came to closing down the activities of Niepokalanow; if all the members of the Militia defected; even if we were scattered like autumn leaves throughout the world – as long as in our souls the ideal of the Militia makes progress and unfolds, then we can boldly claim: *Niepokalanow is making progress.*'

Ivan Vasilievich Moiseyev

1952–1972

The Church has always drawn strength from its martyrs and in early centuries their deaths usually meant public spectacles with sorrowing friends and inquisitive crowds. Today martyrdom often has a special anguish because the blood is shed in an unknown gaol within remote territory and before a few uncaring witnesses.

If death occurs anonymously, particularly in a totalitarian state with government-controlled media and fettered freedoms, some facts are impossible to authenticate. Freedom enables the witness and the evidence which allows martyrdom to be proven. The absence of freedom in Russia means that the truth about the life and death of Vanya – as he was known to family and friends – who died while on National Service with the Soviet Army, remains hidden. Although no doubts seem to exist within the Church of the Reform Baptists in Russia of which he is a martyr, doubts there are. State censorship and stratagems of political expediency are suspect on one side and the tactics of the propaganda of protest on the other.

The following accounts of his story are offered as an illustration of the half-light into which propaganda and secrecy place both the historian and the martyr – for this is how the Reform Baptists now regard Vanya. A hero of the faith is one who lives in the devotion of the people.

The new recruits in Military Unit No. 61968 'T' were given their preliminary briefing at barracks in the Ukrainian seaport of Kerch. The officer told them the city had been established in the sixth century by the Greeks and pointed out the highest hill, named Mithradates, on which still stood the Greek ruins of an acropolis. This, he told the young men, was the seat of the Greek 'soviet'. Warming to his theme, he declared, 'Here the glorious Soviet traditions of human dignity and freedom that only truly began with the Revolution are now carried out under the very shadow of the Greek acropolis.' They were fine sounding words yet at Kerch

Private Ivan ('Vanya') Moiseyev's torments really began.
He had joined up at Odessa some weeks before and already had
a 'record' as a *religioznik*. Religious recruits were regarded as
troublemakers, Baptists particularly; they knew no compromise
and evangelism was all-important to them. Vanya had been late
for roll-call because he had been praying (the soldiers heard the
excuse he gave the sergeant) and the Politicheskoye-Rukovodstvo,
Political Directive Department, had punished him for pro-
selytizing. He scrubbed the enormous barracks drill hall with a
small brush, to teach him 'what knees are for'.

News of his obstinacy at Odessa had reached the Polit-Ruk
Office at Kerch, where Captain Yarmak was determined to change
Vanya's ideas. Yarmak, young and ambitious, wanted to rise in
the system. Every one of the 1100 soldiers on the base had to be
totally committed to the Communist Party and to scientific atheism. 'Until you have a change of mind you'll be confined without
meals,' he told the young Baptist. The boy disconcerted him; he
was not insolent, but strangely unafraid, and his composure
undermined threats.

For five days Vanya went without food and during his fast was
vigorously interrogated by day and night. Sometimes he was ques-
tioned several times in one night. His unit commander, Lieutenant
Colonel V. I. Malsin rebuked the keen young captain in a terse
memo, 'Let Moiseyev eat. I don't wish to be blamed if he dies of
starvation.'

So Captain Yarmak visited Vanya. 'Have you changed your
mind?' he asked. He listened impatiently as the boy told him how
hard he had prayed. 'Suddenly I was warmed and felt as full as if I
had eaten a large and delicious dinner. It is because of God's rescue
that I am not hungry or sick. How can I possibly "change my
mind"?'

Major Gidenko, head of the Polit-Ruk at Kerch, intervened. He
was determined to succeed with young Moiseyev where his sub-
ordinate had failed. The major never had understood the *re-
ligiozniks* in more than thirty years of Army life, and he found it
incredible that a young person, properly educated in socialist
schools, could take such folklore seriously. His experience of deal-
ing with believers had taught him that success owed more to discipline than political re-education, and he confided to his wife, 'I

might as well close down the Polit-Ruk if we had to depend on indoctrination alone.'

When he saw the dangerous *religioznik* he was taken aback. Moiseyev did not look more than sixteen, a simple homesick village lad. The Major adopted a fatherly attitude. 'Missing your family, eh? Do you write home a lot?' Vanya said he had not had much time because of the interrogations. The Major quizzed him, 'You don't accept the principles of scientific atheism upon which are built our entire Soviet State and the strength of the Army?' The boy answered him steadily, 'I cannot accept what I know to be untrue; everything else I can gladly accept.'

The Major began to see what Yarmak had been up against. Yet he persisted, 'But it is not possible to *prove* the existence of God. Why, even your own pastors don't talk as you do about *knowing* God!' He tried a laugh.

The boy's reply dumbfounded him. 'There is no question about knowing him. He is with me now here and on my way over he sent an angel to encourage me.' Was Moiseyev pretending to be *mad*? Trying to work his discharge?

Major Gidenko had heard enough. He decided to discipline Comrade Private Moiseyev by cold. That would give his angel something to do! It was winter with snow lying thickly and swirled into drifts by the icy winds that shrieked around the base. He ordered Moiseyev to stand after lights-out for five hours in the roadway wearing only summer uniform. For twelve consecutive nights, and sometimes for the whole night, the young soldier was so paraded in the sub-zero weather. 'But,' said Vanya, 'I never even felt the cold. If the officers came outside just for ten minutes bundled in great-coats, they would start shivering . . . They would look at me in amazement.'

It was apparent the discipline was ineffective. In fact, Major Gidenko decided the results were far from salutary. The whole base was talking about Moiseyev, and wondering about his God who kept him warm when the temperature was thirty below zero centigrade.

Vanya was luxuriating in his Army bunk as if it were a feather-bed. This night, thankfully, there would be no hours in the snow. He fell asleep before lights-out. Suddenly, he heard the same Voice which had spoken to him on his way to the Major's office, 'Vanya, arise!' He dressed and accompanied his 'angel' through the barracks roof, through time and space to another planet of luminous beauty. Through the 'angel' he communicated with four wondrous 'forms' whom in an extraordinary way he recognized as John the Apostle, David, Moses and Daniel. The 'angel' told him they would fly to another planet in high mountains so that Vanya could glimpse the heavenly city, the New Jerusalem.

Reveillé sounded and the barracks grumbled into life with a cacophony of very human noises – banter, groans and curses. Bemused and fully dressed Vanya longed to re-enter his dream. Then a fellow-Moldavian, who slept next to him, put an extraordinary question. 'Vanya, where did you go last night? I woke about 3 a.m. and your bunk was empty!' Timidly, Vanya asked the duty officer if anyone had left the room during the night. 'Certainly not! Do you want to get me arrested?!'

The young Baptist was popular with his comrades despite his fanciful nonsense about trips with angels and talking gods. There was something attractive about his looks and manner. He had dark, wavy hair and his serious expression was often relieved by a huge smile when the men asked him about his faith. They were curious about his ideas. He was always friendly, industrious, helped anybody. His work records were good and his Colonel gave him grudging credit as an excellent driver (Vanya was continuing his civilian occupation as a chauffeur). He had earned merit points from other officers too. Even in the political classes Vanya had been scrupulous to explain that the Bible taught believers to love their country and to respect the state's authority. He was determined to be a good soldier and worked hard in all aspects of Army life – physical training, drill, military studies, political theory – but his conscientious all-round performance did not protect him from Major Andrei Dolotov.

The Commissar of the Crimean Polit-Ruk, Dolotov, ordered Vanya to be taken from his bed in the middle of one night and put on a train for Sverdlovsk, a military prison in the Urals. When Vanya had been summoned before the Commissar he had told him in his direct fashion, 'I beg of you to understand that I have two sets of loyalties: loyalty to the State and loyalty to God. If I am commanded to do something that would cause me to disobey God, then I am obliged to put my loyalty to him first.'

Within the massive stone walls of the gaunt prison at Sverdlovsk torture cells awaited him. In one, icy water dripped from the ceiling. Another was refrigerated. Once he was put into a pressure suit which near-strangled and half-suffocated him. For twelve days Vanya was exposed to psychological and physical re-education techniques so strenuous that if he were to be kept alive nothing more could be done to him. Finally, the prison authorities decided to send him back to Kerch. They had done their best, and their worst.

*

This version of the first year of Vanya's National Service based on facts the Reform Baptists now believe to be a true record of that time, is vigorously contradicted by the State.

Vanya's eldest brother, Semyon, truck-driver and Party member, called the Bulletin composed by the Council of Churches of Evangelical Christians and Baptists (C.C.E.C.B.) about Vanya's time in the Army a fake document. 'They affirmed that he was persecuted for his faith, he was punished, he was deprived of free time to go to the town, he was tortured. All that is a slander.

'I was honoured to be where my brother served in the Army. I conversed with his commanders and with the soldiers. They had nothing against him. He carried out his duties faithfully ... Within one year of military service he had seven merit points from his C.O. He was twice offered short-term leave home. The Baptists try to persuade people that Vanya was oppressed in the Army. It is not true. I have been in military service myself, and I know that the soldiers are not persecuted, even those who profess religious faith. Vanya had an opportunity to exercise religious ceremonies. For he, like the other soldiers, received passes. In his free time he could go, and he attended prayer meetings.'

In the Soviet newspaper *Literaturnaya Gazeta*, dated November 17, 1976, Boris Roshchin claimed that an inquiry scrutinized Private Moiseyev's daily life during his period of Army training. They examined documents and heard accounts from his colleagues. 'He went nowhere, was arrested by no one, but busied himself with normal military studies.'

Roshchin wrote that Moiseyev had been 'used' for anti-Soviet propaganda to the West, but he remarked that it was worth noting that the radio station, 'Free Europe', *Time* magazine, and other 'instruments of Western propaganda' were 'marvellously restrained' in their descriptions of Moiseyev's 'torture'. A Bulletin of the Reform Baptists, allegedly written in Moiseyev's own words – it is not known to whom, or when – had given details of his ordeals by hunger and cold, and in five special torture cells at Sverdlovsk prison.

The Soviet writer commented, 'It is strange that these weird details are omitted from an article whose subject is "Religious Suppression in the U.S.S.R."! Either they fear that public opinion in the West does not believe tales about Bolshevist commissars eating live children; or they consider that such interfering nonsense in no way discredits the arguments about religious persecution in the U.S.S.R. Either way, the fear is fully justified.'

Roshchin said in his article that for several years before Vanya's conscription into the Army he had, at the insistence of his parents, already belonged to the breakaway group of Baptists. The secretary of this schism was Georgi Vins and Roshchin maintained it was Vins who had spread malicious slander about the Soviet Army and about victimization of members of his sect by means of pre-arranged 'medical certificates' and 'doctor's notes'. Examples of these documents were smuggled abroad where they were utilized as anti-Soviet propaganda.

Boris Roshchin reiterated that 'nobody in the Soviet Union is persecuted for his belief' and accused Vins of disseminating falsehoods which aimed to defile the whole of Soviet society, the Army and the State.

Perhaps in the rest of the 'civilized world', such slander against the State is not actually a crime? Roshchin went on to answer the question he poses. In Great Britain, he alleged, there is a law which states that criminal activity consists of 'deeds done, written or spoken words or manuscripts, pursuing the end of discrediting or evoking indignation against the sovereign, the government, the constitution of the United Kingdom ... or its legal system.' A somewhat contorted proposition, commented a British lawyer, but possibly not totally inaccurate. Roshchin also wrote that the criminal code of the German Federal Republic says that 'he who publicly asserts or disseminates invented or distorted facts, knowing them to be invented or distorted, in order to slander the institution of the State or its decreed supreme bodies . . . is punishable by imprisonment.' It is true that this intention is contained within the criminal code, said an Embassy spokesman, but it is more clearly expressed if the word 'disparage' is used instead of 'slander'.

*

Stories of miracles circulate about Vanya and most are detailed on his tape recordings and in his last letters home. Here is a selection.

When a lecturer on scientific atheism failed to turn up at the base in Kerch for an evening class, the soldiers staged their own debate on the difference between Vanya's God and theirs, which he claimed was the State. A tough Armenian sergeant, Alexandrovich Prokhorov, was in no mood to listen to a lot of preaching from the young Moldavian. He threw down the gauntlet, 'If your God is all-powerful, then let him get me home on leave tomorrow!' Leaves were rare and the men agreed it was a fair challenge to Moiseyev's fairy tales. 'If your God does, then we'll believe in him,' they cried.

Vanya prayed for God's direction. 'Will you be tempted by men? What they ask, is this right?' The answer came, 'Tell them I will do this.'

The next morning he awoke with eager hopes. Instead of morning drill he was ordered into town to pick up the bread for breakfast as there had been no night delivery. He drove into the base an hour later to be met by excited soldiers at the gates. Prokhorov had gone home! A General had telephoned the order from headquarters in Odessa. Major Gidenko had sent soldiers to the station to bring back the sergeant once he heard about the challenge, but they were only in time to see the last carriages disappear into the distance.

That autumn some men from Vanya's unit were sent to Zhostena in the east to help bring in the harvest. The weeks in the open air were a time of spiritual refreshment and rest for Vanya; he was at home here with the evocative smells of the countryside, the sun hot on his back. The harvest was gathered only too soon.

On the journey back to Kerch he was being towed because his Sil-164 had a broken prop-shaft. Suddenly, there was a banging under the towing truck and he sounded the horn to alert the driver. They stopped near the brow of a hill. The men guessed that the universal joint was the cause of the trouble. Vanya crawled under the vehicle with a torch and repair kit.

'I'll just disconnect it. Put the emergency brake on,' he said. He rummaged in his kit for a wrench and succeeded in getting the joint apart. All at once the truck began to roll forward. The truck-driver had not applied the emergency brake. Vanya shouted desperately, 'reverse!' but it was too late.

Doctors were grouped around his bed when he recovered consciousness in the Simferopol Military Hospital. His body burned with fever except for his right arm which was ice cold and without movement. It didn't seem to belong to him. His shallowest breathing plunged him into pain. Vanya prayed, drifted into blackness, prayed again. That evening a surgeon told him they must amputate his right arm and remove part of his crushed lung. A specialist had been summoned. They would operate in the morning.

In an anguish of spirit and body Vanya prayed aloud before the ward and fell asleep in a high fever. At six next morning he awoke to find he could breathe easily, his arm was healed, and his temperature normal.

Hundreds heard about the miraculous healing. Vanya was famous. This was evangelism at its most successful, God triumphant against all human odds. His C.O., Colonel Malsin, raged. That 'fool Surgeon-General' at Simferopol had just telephoned the ludicrous story. 'Colonel, for the first time in my life, I see there really is a God. He has healed Moiseyev. His condition is perfect. We could never have done it.'

Comrade Private Moiseyev was on a bus back to base. The Colonel swore to himself that the Polit-Ruk would be ready for him. Crimean headquarters had issued the order, 'Moiseyev must be broken. There must be no further incidents.' From the moment Vanya unpacked his kit he was interrogated, lectured, cajoled. It seemed that the shouting, the clouting, would never stop. For Vanya the winter was to be one long waking nightmare.

One day early in the following spring, he was driving a van full of bread loaded in trays in the back with the doors bolted and padlocked. An Ukranian sergeant rode with him in the cab.

As Vanya drove he claimed he heard an inner voice telling him,

'Slow down.' The road was clear. The speedometer showed 60 k.p.h. and there seemed no cause for caution. Suddenly, the two men were startled to see loaves rolling along the asphalt at the same speed as the van. They stopped to find half the bread had gone, although the doors were still locked. It took them nearly an hour to recover all the bread and, utterly mystified, they drove on. At the next crossroads they found a coach full of holidaymakers, which had passed them while they were picking up the bread, in collision with a mobile crane. Dead lay everywhere and the burly sergeant was crying.

The Vanya story, according to the Baptists, continues with the conflict of faith affecting both him and his superiors. Colonel Malsin slept badly, smoked to excess, and was plagued with a headache which never left him. The whole Moiseyev business was getting him down. The *religioznik* had a genius for getting publicity out of every bizarre situation. He was an embarrassment, and adept at making his C.O. look foolish.

Despite dedicated efforts to re-educate him, he went on propagating his views. His success with fellow-soldiers was growing. Malsin determined that Moiseyev must be brought to formal trial by Military Tribunal. With only six months left of his compulsory service, the young Baptist must be tried and sentenced before his discharge; but Malsin longed to make him conform. He needed to succeed with Moiseyev to redeem his reputation with his superiors. He dreamed of a public recantation in the Palace of Culture on the base, with Moiseyev begging for the chance to correct the views of comrades he had led into error.

He pressed the bell to summon Comrade Private Moiseyev only to be told that he had been allowed home on leave. When Moiseyev returned there would be a resolution of the problem one way or another, a final outcome. Colonel Malsin had made up his mind.

*

Boris Roshchin wrote that until May 1972, when his 'distinct success' during his military training allowed him to be released to take 'leave', Moiseyev had spoken to no one either about the 'miracles' that had occurred or about any kind of persecution. At home, according to his father, he told them that everything was all right in his section, and that he was respected and praised. He was even driver for the commander of his section, and the Army let him go to prayer meetings. Then Roshchin described how Moiseyev met activists from the C.C.E.C.B. 'What they talked about is not known, but back he went to his section, taking with him the address of the "leader" of the Reform Baptists, Vasilii Miroshnichenko.'

Roshchin went on, 'In the simplicity of her soul, Miroshnichenko's wife told us: "He was a saint, was Brother Vanya, actually holy, and we said as much to him several times." '

Roshchin pressed the point. 'A *saint*. And what sort of saint would he be without a crown of thorns and a martyr's death? The C.C.E.C.B. at that time could well do with their very own saint. Faith was weakening, and it was not necessarily because of "persecution on the part of the authorities".' Here Roshchin quoted from leaflets purported to be published by the Reform Baptists. ' "In our days of inactivity, the majority of believers is defeated . . . Our eagerness to believe is not enough . . . In our age man has fallen from God . . ." How all this was needed, just as the C.C.E.C.B. needed its saint!'

The role of martyr fitted Moiseyev like a glove, Roschin declared. 'A man not lacking in ability, he quickly adopted the ingenuous fundamentals as presented in his community training: he must suffer and believe, believe and suffer. Of necessity, he learned the dictum, "Nothing venture, nothing gain." Youth, like a bunch of fresh roses, gives his life in atonement. He awaits the reward due to Christ's martyr.' Moiseyev had read the 139 tales contained in the fat little volume *The Children's Friend*, published by the C.C.E.C.B., many of which described the death in reward for faith of near ones and dear ones, and the suffering which genuine Christians must accept.

Miroshnichenko, the Baptist leader, not only took Moiseyev to his house, but also visited him back with his unit during the summer 'as a representative of Christ', and before long the 'martyrdom' would happen by the sea. Semyon Moiseyev (Vanya's eldest brother and the only member of the family of seven boys and a girl to join Komsomol, the junior Communist league) told Roschchin that shortly before Vanya died, he wrote in his diary: 'State orders: go into the sea and return. Christ's orders: go into the sea and do not return.'

Roschchin asked, 'Who gave Moiseyev God's orders? Surely not the angels!' Semyon Moiseyev said, 'I cannot get rid of the idea that the whole story of Vanya's death is the invention of the breakaway Baptists.'

*

According to the Reform Baptists, Vanya spent the last days of his leave recording the chill details of his trials in the Army on a tape machine brought to the Moiseyevs' cottage in Volontirovka by a fellow Baptist. Tape recorders and microphones were incongruous modern phenomena in the modest village; but for some years Brother Zheluak from the Slabodzeya congregation had taped the Christian broadcasts he picked up on his shortwave radio. Now the wonderful deeds God had wrought for Vanya could be relayed to congregations all over Moldavia; not only the believers in their own region of Suvorovskiy would hear about them.

In 1972 spring came to the pleasant and serene countryside with an almost unbearable beauty. Or so it seemed to Vanya. This was the trick spring always played, he told himself; its loveliness was an annual miracle. He loved his home. He knew each tree, every secret path, the places where birds chose to nest, where to look for mushrooms. His eyes searched the familiar scene so as to preserve it in loving detail to see in his mind's eye when back with his unit and facing yet sterner trials. Vanya knew he would not see Moldavia again.

The military prosecutor in Simferopol warmed up the same accusations that Vanya had heard many times before from the Polit-Ruk. Under Article 142 he was charged with being a member of an unregistered Baptist congregation in Moldavia.

The sect to which Vanya belonged broke away from the official Baptist body, the All-Union Council of Evangelical Christians and Baptists (A.U.C.E.C.B.) in 1965, and exists to this day in a technically illegal condition. It calls itself the Council of Churches of Evangelical Christians and Baptists (C.C.E.C.B.) and its leaders call for uncompromising loyalty to Christ, for continual spiritual renewal and for evangelism. They also lobby for justice for Soviet believers and are active in the wider Soviet human rights movement. The Reform Baptists are the only Christians in Russia to produce lists of members in prison and give addresses of labour camps. They also operate a secret printing press. They broke away from the main stream because they were disenchanted by what they saw as an unholy pact between their formal Church body and the atheist State.

The State under Khrushchev had succeeded in making the Church stage a charade in which it seemed willing to sign its own death-warrant. Incredibly, two documents which undermined the very foundations of Christian life in Russia were adopted in 1960 by the All-Union Council: a set of 'New Statutes' for the Baptist Church and a 'Letter of Instructions' circulated to all senior presbyters. The full text has never been published but quotations reveal its attack to be focussed particularly on Christian work among the young. Children were to be excluded from services, and both the baptisms of young people and evangelistic teaching were to be severely discouraged. Only those congregations which had been subservient enough to gain registration from the civil authorities could be recognized by the All-Union Council. This made it appear as if the official Baptist body endorsed the discrimination, and often illegality, of the State's action over registration.

While the All-Union Council may have made backstage representations to the Government, they never publicly justified their adoption of these documents, although they tried to mitigate their apparent collusion by saying that the statutes were introduced only experimentally. They were an embarrassment and after three years the Letter of Instructions was cancelled and the New Statutes modified.

The basic Soviet legislation on religion is the Law on Religious Associations of 1929 which was only slightly amended in 1932. In 1975 the Soviet Government announced revisions of the 1929 legislation affecting nearly half of the Law's sixty-eight articles. Some experts say some aspects of registration have become more oppressive and that the revised law reflects a hardening of the line against believers; others point to more optimistic signs of improved relations between State and Church.

Today in the West it is hard to discover the truth about religious freedom in Russia. The law is obscure and the loopholes are many. There is often a quixotic application or violation of the law. Nevertheless, the degree of State interference in the internal affairs of the Church seems excessive and unwarrantable both in law and practice. The claim of the Soviet State that it does not interfere in the internal religious affairs of the Church is irreconcilable with legislation which is quite specific about the limits set for religious activity. Registration of buildings for worship is required but it is neither automatic nor simple. The Reform Baptists do not accept the Soviet laws about registered buildings and so are often sent to prison. They are being punished not because they are Christians, the authorities maintain, but for defying these regulations. On the other hand the schismatic Baptists regard the enforcement of such laws as improper interference in church matters.

Apart from membership of an unregistered congregation, Moiseyev was also charged by the Military Prosecutor with attending unregistered meetings in Kerch during hours intended for his relaxation. He was further accused of distributing literature libellous of the Soviet State. A letter to his parents was produced saying that he was 'suffering for Christ'.

The Tribunal officer read from The Decree of Lenin, Point 5: 'Free celebration of religious rites is guaranteed insofar as they do not disturb public order and do not infringe the rights of citizens of the Soviet Republic.'

The prosecuting officer, his face a stone, eyed Vanya closely. 'Comrade Moiseyev, you have infringed the rights of your fellow-soldiers in your unit and company and in other units with which you have had contact,' he declared. 'Your continuous observance of prayer and preaching are intolerable to others around you. You have been repeatedly ordered to desist from this harassment of others but have refused. Your religious observations on State property have violated the regulations on the separation of Church and State.'

Vanya was given the opportunity during the next three days to confess his anti-Soviet activity and publicly to change his views.

There followed for him a fortnight of moves between prisons and the Tribunal and the base at Kerch. He constantly reiterated his innocence and told Commissar Dolotov, 'I have never harassed others with the preaching of the gospel. Where there has been interest I have spoken of the love of God. I don't consider it a crime to give bread to the hungry. The only religious observance in which I have engaged on the base is prayer and what law forbids Soviet citizens to pray? You tell me not to talk about my faith but the love of God cannot be hidden.'

For ten days after this exchange Vanya was severely punished in the prison security cells. The Military Tribunal then refused to continue. 'In our judgement persuasive efforts are futile. This prisoner can be quickly sentenced and sent away.' After a few days Moiseyev was sent back to Kerch where he was placed in special quarters and given a last deadline by which to change his mind.

On the morning of July 16, 1972, Colonel Malsin had to conduct Party officials from Yugoslavia around the base and it was noon before he could get away. K.G.B. (secret police) officers were waiting in his office. Moiseyev was detailed to drive himself to the K.G.B. headquarters in the city as if on an ordinary assignment. Malsin and the civilian security officers would leave the base in another car.

The K.G.B. experts in the sound-proof room were no more successful than the Polit-Ruk and the Military Tribunal in making Moiseyev deny his God. The difference was that their efforts were conclusive. Theirs was the final brutality. The security police did not think the inert body on the stone floor was yet dead. Comrade Private Moiseyev's death could be arranged as an accident. Gulls flying over the Black Sea cried as if in protest.

The death certificate (No. 2860641) cited 'mechanical asphyxiation from drowning'. Vanya's letters from barracks told of 'torments and trials' as a Christian and during his recent leave he had spoken of the fearful details, but a telegram from the Colonel to his parents said, 'Your son has been tragically killed.'

The report of a 'drowning accident' struck a false note; and his mother wanted to dress the body in civilian clothes, as was their right. She insisted that the Army seals should be broken and the coffin opened. The soldiers who had brought it to the front parlour of the cottage at Volontirovka left abruptly, making their excuses that other duties called them away. Then, as Vanya's father, Vasiliiy Trofimovich, began to lever open the casket with a crowbar, his eldest son, Semyon, the only Party member in the family, made frenzied attempts to stop him. Semyon was pulled away by pastors, and when the lid was raised anguish transfixed the faces of everyone who looked.

Momentarily Joanna Konstantinova lied to herself: the body belonged to an older worn man, whose face was hideously bruised as if from a despairing struggle. The mouth was swollen, oddly misshapen. His forehead and the sides of his head were blackened and bore grotesque lumps. Then grief tore into her like a wild animal; there was no doubt, it was her own dear Vanya.

The boy's confident words on his last night at home rang in her mind. 'The Lord has told me to speak for him wherever I am and not to be silent.' He had just returned from a farewell meeting, someone's birthday had provided the official excuse. Many young people had been there and he told her happily, 'Stefan (a friend) spoke of this tonight – that we are all to preach the gospel wherever we are, in school, in our work, wherever, following the example of the prophets and apostles.'

The family and friends of the young soldier were now certain he had been murdered by torture for the candour of his religious beliefs. The Moiseyevs protested to the world.

Their letter went to A. A. Grechko, Minister of the Armed Forces, U.S.S.R., and to Leonid I. Brezhnev, General Secretary of the Central Committee of the Communist Party of the Soviet Union. It reached the Union of Writers of the U.S.S.R., the U.S.S.R. Academy of Sciences, and leading newspapers.

Copies went to the Council of Churches of Evangelical Christians and Baptists, and the Council of Prisoners' Relatives in the U.S.S.R., a group formed in the early sixties for the defence of men and women imprisoned for actions prompted by their Christian beliefs.

Their protest went abroad to Kurt Waldheim, Secretary General of the United Nations, and the International Committee for the Defence of Human Rights at the United Nations. The letter, dated August 1, 1972, was also addressed simply, 'To All Christians.'

It claimed that their son had been killed during torture for his faith in God, and called for a prompt investigation and an autopsy by a medical team to include two local Christian doctors. A statement accompanied the letter signed by twenty-three witnesses present at Vanya's funeral, contending that death occurred as a result of premeditated violence. 'We confirm this with photographs and facts: the heart was punctured six times, the legs and

the head were severely beaten, and there were burns on the chest.'
Both believers and unbelievers had signed.

*

An undated letter (published in *Vanya* by Myrna Grant) gives an
eye-witness account of the accident by L. A. Martinenko of
Stavropola, who claims to have been with friends in the military
car driven by Moiseyev, and commandeered by a Soviet officer
who wanted 'to show us the sights of the Crimea'. They drove to
the Cape of Borzovka. It became very hot and they decided to
swim. The military officer told the children with them, and the
driver, 'Don't rush into the water. First cool off, then go in to
swim.' Later he said to Moiseyev, 'Dive in and have a swim but
come straight back to the car. We'll be going on soon.' Soon one of
the party came running to Martinenko who had stayed on the
beach, and shouted, 'Our driver has drowned!' The officer swam
looking for him but after ten minutes a wave brought the body to
the surface. Martinenko went for an ambulance. Meanwhile a
doctor from nearby tried artificial respiration, massaged with al-
cohol, applied mustard plasters, injected. For three hours they
worked to resuscitate the young soldier and about fifty people
were on the scene.

*

A letter (undated) from Vanya's brother, Semyon, claimed to
refute the Bulletin published by the Reform Baptists purporting to
give the facts. Semyon wrote, 'The so-called brothers in Christ set
up a wail through nearly the entire world, maintaining that
Vanya suffered for the cause of his belief, that he was drowned by
force. I cannot be silent, when some people talk all kind of nonsense, threaten our Soviet rules, and throw shadows on the Soviet
people ...' The Baptists lied. He had talked to those who were
present. His brother drowned by accident. It could happen to
anybody.

His letter went on, 'We brought my brother's body home in a
coffin made of zinc. Here I understood that the Baptists' leaders
were plotting something. They decided to take pictures. They
pushed me away from the coffin; there were many of them in the
house. At the funeral, the Baptists put a blank sheet of paper in

front of the fool countrymen to get them to sign their names. People did so, without thinking that later, above their names, the Baptists' leaders would stage an "act" in which they maintain that Vanya's death was caused as a result of premeditated murder. What a dishonest counterfeit!

'Who did it? So-called Baptists, and, above all, their leaders. Vanya used to meet with these illegal servants of God but he did not tell them that he had taken the military oath.'

Conscientious objectors are sentenced under Article 249a of the Criminal Code, which states that 'evasion of military duties by self-infliction of injuries or by simulation of illness, forgery of documents or other deception, and also by refusal to perform military duties' is punishable by deprivation of liberty for three to seven years. But refusal to take the military oath is not mentioned in Article 249a, and most objectors are prepared to perform non-combatant duties. In spite of this, however, it is argued in appeal cases that since military regulations do not allow a soldier who has not taken the oath to be allocated any duties, refusal to take the oath is tantamount to refusal to perform military duties.

Semyon Moiseyev did not blame his parents for 'the letter which accused honest people', but the leaders of the Reform Baptists who composed it for them. ('Yes, my parents are Christian, but they will never get involved in dirty business; they will never slander our people or our governmental system.') He had these words for the schismatic Baptists: 'Your Bulletin is a fraud. It is needed by the leadership who give you orders from abroad. I know that the slanderous information about Vanya's death was translated into many languages, multiplied, and spread into fifteen countries.'

*

A Commission of Inquiry visited Volontirovka in mid-September, 1972, fifty-two days after the burial. They began by cross-examining each villager who had signed the funeral document and every non-Christian withdrew his or her testimony that Vanya's death was the result of premeditated violence. The next day Vanya's body was exhumed; but only his parents and one brother were allowed to watch. The Commission did not include Christian doctors as requested. The heart and surrounding tissues were excised before reburial of the body. No report from the Commission has been published.

*

Nearly six months after the incident, a News Agency release printed in many Russian papers, gave this account (January 5, 1973):

On a hot July day in 1972 a soldier named Ivan Moiseyev drowned approximately a hundred metres from shore at Cape Borzovka near the city of Kerch. Many were in the water with him, so the man was quickly dragged to the shore. Everything possible was done to save him. At first artificial respiration was administered. Later, after indirect massage of the heart, Dr. E. Novikovno injected adrenalin into the heart and ofedrin into a vein. However, the struggle for life was in vain, and the following autopsy showed that he was drowned, with paralysis of the heart following immediately.

The death of the young man was taken very hard by his comrades in the service, but it never entered their minds that this unfortunate accident would be used by base people who counted Moiseyev as their 'brother'. Among his relatives there turned out to be Evangelical Christians/Baptists. The leaders of the C.C.E.C.B. decided to use the death of their 'brother' to stir up trouble. They told those who gathered at his funeral in the village of Volontirovka (Moldavia) that he was 'tortured'. The marks on his body were from the attempts to save his life and from the autopsy, but they were falsely interpreted as evidence of horrible tortures. At the funeral the mischief-makers obtained a collection of signatures to a slanderous 'document'.

Four years later Boris Roshchin wrote in *Literaturnaya Gazeta* (17.11.76) that he had discovered the truth. He ruled out both accidental drowning and death by torture. The Reform Baptists badly needed a holy martyr for propaganda purposes and this idealistic youth had been persuaded to fill the role and to commit suicide in the sea. His death had, in fact, been stage-managed by fellow-Christians. Roshchin claimed he had investigated the incident and talked to most of the people involved.

Roshchin's version went like this. In July 1972, while bathing not far from the shore in the Sea of Azov, Moiseyev drowned under the eyes of numerous other bathers. Attempts to revive him proved futile, despite on-the-spot treatment and first-aid by doctors from a nearby holiday hotel.

The Reform Baptists protested that the body bore evidence of torture. Their charge was dismissed by Roshchin who attributed the puncture wounds near the heart to traces of intracardial adrenalin injections given by a doctor, Irina Novikova, in an attempt to resuscitate the man. The drowning, contended Roshchin, was deliberate. This poetic young man had agreed to be Christ's martyr in a plot invented by Georgi Vins the secretary of the schismatic Baptists (who was released from prison on April 28, 1979, and flown to New York with four others in exchange for two Soviet spies; Vins does not view this as freedom but expulsion). According to eye-witnesses, wrote Roshchin, Moiseyev did not cry 'Help!', or 'I'm drowning!' Instead he shouted a joyous exclamation, something like 'Hallelujah!' before he sank under the waves.

Georgi Vins was alleged by Roshchin to have made capital for the Christian cause from the soldier's death. He had prepared a photomontage on which could be seen 'traces of martyrdom' and the 'fatal blows' dealt to Moiseyev. He now capped his earlier stories of 'miracles and tortures' with other 'less funny and more spiteful inventions'. Vins alleged, wrote Roschin, that officers, seeing Moiseyev's steadfastness, 'slaughtered' him, took the corpse away in a car with the word 'truth' emblazoned on it, and threw him into the sea in broad daylight, in front of witnesses!

*

Three months later (March 5, 1976) an open letter was received by Boris Roshchin from 674 members of the Reform Baptists in the town of Kharkov. Their letter was also addressed to L. I. Brezhnev, and copies were sent to the editors of *Literaturnaya Gazeta*, and *Radayanska Ukraine*. It reached The Council of Prisoners' Relatives and greeted 'All Baptists'.

The believers accused Roschin of using his prominent position in the State 'not only to pour a bucket of slops over the believers, but to lay their fire with damp and sappy brushwood, namely, the invented cause of Moiseyev's death.' His article had been widely reprinted, and had also stimulated a plethora of similar newspaper features.

The Baptists posed these questions. Can a man, swimming in shallow waters not far from the shore, really shout suddenly not

'I'm drowning', not 'Help!' but something joyful like 'Hallelujah!', sink beneath the water without anyone's help, but using only his own strength of will, hold his breath and die? How does Roschin explain that an underwater expert found no water in the lungs of the corpse, although the body had been in the water for more than twenty minutes? How too does he explain that marks on the body were reminiscent of heel prints and perforations by a sharp object? Surely no doctor would leave marks which could be taken for torture?

'How are we to believe that martial atheists took no part in the death of Moiseyev and others, when today we have a Stalinist constitution in power, and the attitude towards believers is now as it was in the 1930s, when churches and prayer houses suddenly emptied, and believers all at once changed from being exemplary citizens into enemies of the people, agents of imperialism?'

During the war years the Soviet State made a tenuous truce with the churches so that members might be galvanized to the cause of patriotism. Concessions were made privately between Stalin and some of the Church leaders which led to a relaxation of pressure and to a religious renaissance.

Repression returned after the struggle had ended, and when Khrushchev became first secretary of the All-Union Party on the death of Stalin in 1953, he began a new war against religion as 'a bourgeois survival'. Congregations had their property expropriated and the most influential pastors were removed from their pulpits.

The Reform Baptists ridiculed Boris Roschin's version of the death of 'The Young People's Martyr' as Vanya came to be called. 'Baptists do not make human sacrifices,' they declared. 'Torturers make martyrs.'

Epilogue

The word 'martyr', in its original sense of witness to Christ, has a legendary ring about it, reminiscent of amphitheatre and pyre. It was perilous to be a Christian in early centuries and when I realized that for many it still is today, I resolved to write this book.

Perhaps not since Roman times has there been such conflict between Church and State, idealist and materialist. The old word martyr retains a glorious relevance. Countless Christians of our time die in defence of their faith and such sacrifice must be a cause for rejoicing and thanksgiving. Their example gives encouragement and inspiration to succeeding generations of believers. Faithfulness unto death may still be asked of Christians, and we are surrounded in our daily pilgrimage by a growing 'cloud of witnesses' who support us on our way.

I have also written this book for the unbeliever, that he may look again at this man, who, lifted up, has had the power to draw so many after him. And that seeing, he too may believe.

Acknowledgements

This book was made possible by the families, friends and colleagues of the martyrs. They gave me interviews, written accounts, cherished letters, diaries, cassettes, maps and photographs. I owe them all my deepest thanks. I list their names alphabetically with the sources for each chapter.

I much appreciate the Foreword contributed by the Right Rev. Leslie Brown.

I am grateful to those authors and publishers who gave me permission to quote from their works.

I am also indebted to the Rev. Neville Cryer, director, Bible Society, and to librarians: Mrs D. G. Brewster U.S.P.G.; Mrs. B. L. Hough, former archivist U.S.P.G.; Miss Jean M. Woods, C.M.S.; Mr. A. R. B. Fuller, St. Paul's Cathedral; Mr. Michael Gibson, Avon Country Reference; Martin Purvis and my youngest son, Stephen, Bristol Grammar School. Most of all, thanks go to my husband, James, for his help and encouragement.

Pictures

Janani Luwum, C.M.S., London; Helmuth James von Moltke, Mrs. Freya von Moltke; Andrew Kaguru, Pastor Samuel Muhoro; Vivian Redlich, the Rev. Anthony Neal; May Hayman, Mrs. E. R. Hayman; Daw Pwa Sein, Daw Aye Sein; Roger Youderian, Auca Missionary Foundation; Toña, Barbara Youderian and Summer Institute of Linguistics, Ecuador; Martinez Quintana, the Rev. Clyde W. Taylor; Maximilian Kolbe, The Crusade of Mary Immaculate; and Ivan Vasilievich Moiseyev, Keston College, the Centre for the Study of Religion and Communism.

Maps

The Most Rev. George Appleton, Canon Edward Kelly, the Rev. Clyde W. Taylor, Mrs Ethel Wallis and Messrs. Hodder & Stoughton.

Sources

JANANI LUWUM

Christians in Contact No. 122, March 1977.
Church of England Newspaper, February 25, 1977.
C.M.S. News Special No. 12, 1977.
C.H.S. News Special No. 12, 1977.
C.M.S. Yes Magazine, April–June 1977.
Daily Telegraph, February 18, March 21, 1977.
Ford, Margaret, *Janani* (Marshall Morgan & Scott, 1977).
Guardian, February 17, 18, 22, March 31, 1977.
Kivengere, Bishop Festo, with Smoker, Dorothy, *I love Idi Amin* (Marshall Morgan & Scott, 1977).
Kyemba, Henry, *State of Blood* (Transworld Publishers Ltd, in association with Paddington Press, Corgi edition, 1977).
Life of Faith, February 26, 1977.
Observer, February 20, May 1, 1977.
Parish Magazine of St. Peter's Church, Harrogate, March 1977.
Pirouet, Louise, *Strong in the Faith* (Church of Uganda Literature Centre, 1969).
Sunday Telegraph, February 20, April 3, 1977.
Sunday Times, February 20, March 6, June 5, June 12, 1977.
The Times, February 21, 1977.
Many friends and brother-bishops of Janani Luwum, both in Uganda and England.

HELMUTH JAMES VON MOLTKE

Balfour, Michael, and Frisby, Julian, *Helmuth von Moltke. A Leader Against Hitler* (Macmillan, 1972).
Gollwitzer, Hellmut, Kuhn, Kathe, and Schneider, Reinhold (eds.), *Dying We Live* (Harvill Press Ltd., 1956; Fontana Books, 1958).
Moltke, Helmuth, *A German of the Resistance: The Last Letters of Count Helmuth James von Moltke* (Oxford University Press, 1948).
Professor Michael Balfour, Mr. John Gwynne, Mrs. Freya von Moltke, Rev. Edwin Robertson.

ANDREW KAGURU

Bewes, Canon T. F. C., *Kikuyu Conflict* (The Highway Press, 1953).
Bewes, Canon T. F. C., *The Work of the Christian Church among the Kikuyu* (International Affairs, Vol. XXIX No. 3, July 1953).

Carothers, Dr. J. C., *The Psychology of Mau Mau* (The Government Printer, Nairobi, 1954).

C.M.S. Pamphlet, *Mau Mau – What is it?* (C.M.S., 1952).

Corfield, F. D., *Historical Survey of the Origins and Growth of Mau Mau* (H.M.S.O., 1960).

Daily Telegraph, August 23, 1978.

Kenyatta, Jomo, *Facing Mount Kenya* (Martin Secker & Warburg Ltd., 1938).

Leakey, I. S. B., *Mau Mau and the Kikuyu* (Methuen & Co. Ltd., 1952).

Wiseman, E. M., *Kikuyu Martyrs* (The Highway Press, 1958).

Canon Cecil Bewes, Mr. Cyril Hooper, Mr. Danson Kaguru, Mrs. Mollie MacKenzie, Pastor Samuel Muhoro.

VIVIAN REDLICH AND MAY HAYMAN

Dusen, Henry P. Van, *They Found the Church There* (S.C.M. Press, 1945).

Henrich, Ruth, *Heroes of the Church Today* (S.P.G., 1948).

Mayo, Lida, *Bloody Buna* (Australian National University Press, 1975).

Rowland, E. C., *Faithful unto Death* (Australian Board of Missions, 1967).

Strong, P. N. W., *Out of Great Tribulation* (The Presidential Address and Charge of the Bishop of New Guinea to his Diocesan Conference at Dogura, June 30, 1947).

Rt. Rev. Jeremy Ashton, Canon John Bodger, Miss I. M. Brooksbank, Canon R. L. Butterss, Canon J. Clayton, contemporaries at the Theological College, Chichester, Most Rev. David Hand, Mrs. E. R. Hayman, Canon Edward Kelly, Rev. Anthony Neal, Mr. Christopher J. Walker.

DAW PWA SEIN

Appleton, George, *The War and After* series, No. 1, *Burma* (S.P.G., 1946).

Arnold-Forster, Mark, *The World at War* (Collins, 1973).

Chapman, Josephine, *Brave Christians of Burma* (S.P.G., 1946).

Chapman, Josephine, *Weathering the Storm* (S.P.G., 1946).

Collier, Basil, *A Short History of the Second World War* (Collins, 1967).

Encyclopaedia Brittanica.

Hart, Basil Liddell, *History of the Second World War* (Book Club Associates, by arrangement with Cassell, 1973).

Henrich, Ruth, *Heroes of the Church Today* (S.P.G., 1948).

Jesse, F. Tennyson, *The Story of Burma* (Macmillan, 1946).

Most Rev. George Appleton, Naw Esther Tun Hlaing, Mrs. Christopher

Lewis (née Chapman), Miss Dorothy Lewis, Mrs. Iris Scott (née Miller), Daw Aye Sein, Most Rev. George West and Mrs. West.

ROGER YOUDERIAN AND TOÑA

Elliot, Elisabeth, *Through Gates of Splendour* (Harper and Row Publishers Inc., 1975).
Wallis, Ethel, *Aucas Downriver* (Hodder & Stoughton, 1973).
Wallis, Ethel, *In Other Words* (Wycliffe Publications, Jan. 1976).
Wycliffe Translation Magazines, excerpts 1969–1972.
Gospel Missionary Union, Mrs. Elisabeth Elliot Leitch, Missionary Aviation Fellowship, Dr. Catherine Peeke, Dr. and Mrs. Abe Van Der Puy, Señor Washington Padilla J., Summer Institute of Linguistics, Wycliffe Bible Translators, Mr. John H. Twentyman.

MARTINEZ QUINTANA

Encyclopaedia Brittanica, 1974.
Ordonez, Francisco, *Historia del Cristianismo Evangelico* (La Tipografia Union de Medellín, Colombia).
Sunday Times Magazine, 'Planet Earth, No. 1, Colombia.'
Señor Alberto Carcamo C., Rev. George S. Constance, Señor Alfonso Corzo C., Rev. R. Wesley Perry, Rev. Dr. Clyde W. Taylor.

MAXIMILIAN KOLBE

Bar, Prof. Father Gioacchino, *The Death of Blessed Maximilian Kolbe in the light of the canon law* (Milizia dell'Immacolata, Rome).
Burdyszek, John Maria, O.F.M.Conv., *Crusade of Mary Immaculate in England* (Crusade of Mary Immaculate Press, Manchester).
Cooper, R. W., *The Nuremberg Trial* (Penguin Books, 1947).
Domanski, Father Giorgio M., O.F.M.Conv., *The Cities of the Immaculate in the World* (Miles Immaculatae, 1977).
Domanski, Father Giorgio M., O.F.M.Conv., *The historic data about the life of Father Maximilian Kolbe* (Milizia dell'Immacolata, Rome).
Graef, Hilda, *Mystics of our Times* (Burns and Oates, 1962).
Kolbe, Maximilian Maria, *Maria was his middle Name: Day by day with Blessed Maximilian Maria Kolbe*, Jerzy M. Domanski, compiler, Regis N. Barwig, translator (The Benziger Sisters Publishers, 1977).
Winowska, Maria, *The Death Camp Proved Him Real* (Prow Books/ Franciscan Marytown Press, 1971).
Fr. John Burdyszek, O.F.M.Conv., Fr. Giorgio M. Domanski, O.F.M.Conv., Fr. Gerard McCann, O.F.M.Conv.

IVAN ('VANYA') VASILIEVICH MOISEYEV

Bourdeaux, Michael, *Faith on Trial in Russia* (Hodder and Stoughton, 1971).

Bourdeaux, Michael, and Murray, Katharine, *Young Christians in Russia* (Marshall Morgan and Scott, 1976).

Grant, Myrna, *Vanya* (Creation House, Carol Stream, Illinois 60187, 1974).

Keston News Service, *Newsletter, July 28, 1977* (Keston College, Centre for the Study of Religion and Communism).

Kharkov Believers, *Open Letter to Boris Roshchin*, March 5, 1977.

Roshchin, Boris, article Nov. 17, 1976, in *Literaturnaya Gazeta*.

Sawatsky, Walter, article entitled 'The New Soviet Law on Religion' in *Religion in Communist Lands*, Vol. 4 No. 2, Summer 1976 (Keston College).

Miss Jane Ellis.

The Concise Oxford Dictionary of the Christian Church

Edited by Elizabeth A. Livingstone

The range of the *Concise Dictionary* is considerable. It covers the major Christian feasts and denominations and includes accounts of the lives of the saints, résumés of Patristic writings, histories of heretical sects, and outlines of the opinions of major theologians and moral philosophers. Many related subjects are also explored in this comprehensive work: there are entries on painters, sculptors, and composers; non-Christian religions and rituals; famous cathedrals; and significant discoveries in textual criticism and archaeology.

Aquinas

Anthony Kenny

Anthony Kenny writes about Thomas Aquinas as a philosopher, for readers who may not share Aquinas's theological interests and beliefs. He begins with an account of Aquinas's life and works, and assesses his importance for contemporary philosophy. The book is completed by more detailed examinations of Aquinas's metaphysical system and his philosophy of mind.

Past Masters
Published in the U.S.A. by Hill & Wang

Persecution in the Early Church

by Herbert A. Workman

Persecution of the Church is now more widespread
than it has ever been, yet the proud boast of Tertullian,
with which Dr Workman ends his book, can still be
justified: 'The blood of the martyrs is indeed the seed
of the Church. Dying we conquer. The moment we
are crushed, that moment we go forth victorious'.

No book portrays more graphically for the general
reader the sufferings of the martyrs of the first
Christian centuries than *Persecution in the Early
Church*, which was originally published in 1906 and
has since achieved the status of a classic.

Jesus

Humphrey Carpenter

Humphrey Carpenter writes about Jesus from the standpoint of a historian coming fresh to the subject without religious preconceptions. He examines the reliability of the Gospels, the originality of Jesus's teaching, and Jesus's view of himself. His highly readable book achieves a remarkable degree of objectivity about a subject which is deeply embedded in Western culture.

Past Masters

Published in the U.S.A. by Hill & Wang

Edmund Campion

Evelyn Waugh

Edmund Campion (1540–1581) was destined for the highest offices in the University of Oxford, where he was a brilliant scholar, and in the Church of England. However, his conviction that the Church of Elizabeth and Cecil was a betrayal of catholicism grew steadily, and he resolved to go on foot to Rome as a pilgrim and to become a Jesuit. He slipped back to England in disguise and preached daringly to secret assemblies of Catholics. He was captured and hanged, drawn, and quartered in 1581.

Evelyn Waugh's Life is a model for hagiographers; historically sound, matching Campion's own prose, it has established itself as a classic.

Christianity and the World Order

E. R. Norman, Dean of Peterhouse, Cambridge

This book, based on Dr Norman's 1978 Reith Lectures, considers a subject of great topical significance: the implications of the contemporary politicization of Christianity. Ranging from the political radicalism of Latin American Marxist Christians to the problems encountered by Christianity in the Soviet Union, Dr Norman identifies and presents a critical analysis of the social and political ideas to which the modern Church is attaching itself.